P9-ECR-068

6.60

THOMAS F. McGANN, s.j.

Ethics: Theory and Practice

LOYOLA UNIVERSITY PRESS

Chicago, Illinois   60657

© 1971 Loyola University Press

Printed in the United States of America
Library of Congress Catalog Card Number: 73-156370
ISBN 0-8294-0202-0

About this book

Ethics: Theory and Practice was designed by William Nicoll of Edit, Inc. It was set in the composing room of Loyola University Press. The text is 12/14 Bodoni Book; the reduced matter, 10/12; the notes, 8/10. The display type is 12 Bodoni Book caps.

It was printed by Photopress, Inc., on Warren's 60-pound English Finish paper and bound by The Engdahl Company in Bancroft cloth.

BJ
1012
.M317 21,068

CONTENTS

Modern science has placed in our hands fantastically effective instruments for controlling nature, and in doing so has vastly increased the complexity of leading an ethical life. It has given women the Pill which enables them to control ovulation and limit births, only to occasion the question, Is it *right* to do so? The Bomb empowers the nation that has it to wreak havoc upon its enemies. The problem is, May it be used for such a purpose?

These and a host of other moral issues are now being hotly discussed. Strangely enough, it is from the younger generation that one hears the most moral discourse. Though their elders stigmatize them for their use of drugs, sexual license, and espousal of a new morality which sounds very much like the old immorality, they are in fact keenly sensitive to the moral point of view: the wrongness of war, racial discrimination, pharisaism, and dishonesty in all its forms. Situation ethics, with its thesis that only love matters, has a strong appeal for them. The bare possibility that they may be on to something is suggested by the quite remarkable concern for one another's welfare they exhibited at the Woodstock, New York, music festival. The local sheriff remarked they were the "nicest bunch of kids" he had ever met.

Traditional morality has lost these young people—"turned them off," as they say. If it is to be made relevant to them, morality must be rethought; apriorism must yield to the facts of the human situation; the old absolutes must be reexamined in terms of changing circumstances. Whatever is of value in the new approach should be acknowledged and adopted in the making of a new synthesis.

Our book attempts to make some advances in this direction. Though Thomistic in its basic orientation, it pays respectful attention to the views of the great nonscholastic philosophers. We have found particular merit in Kant's contention that the moral law is the absolute and immutable imperative of reason. We have learned much from what Schlick, Campbell, and Nowell-Smith said about free will, from the Ayer-Toulmin debate on the intelligibility of moral terms, and Philippa Foot's critique of Moore's "naturalistic fallacy."

We have dealt not only with the theoretical side of ethics but also with the practical. We have treated the moral problems which confront the individual: the possibility of ignorance of the moral law, the problem of the erroneous conscience, the certitude required for morally permissible action. On the social level we have discussed the dilemma of the legislator: when he may yield to what James called "social pressure," when he must stand firm on moral principle.

On the whole, our effort has been to be brief and to the point. Aware that the college student's desire to learn the moral point of view on the issues confronting society today does not usually include any consuming ambition to become a professional ethician, we have tried to be as succinct as possible. For those who would like to explore them in greater depth we have provided copious references.

FREE WILL

Free will is a prerequisite for morality. *Ought* implies *can*. It is pointless to talk of what man ought to do unless he is the responsible author of his acts, able to set his own course, to do or not to do as he chooses. Some discussion of this fundamental question will be in order, then, as we begin the study of ethics.

It is of course not possible to prove that man is free. The verifiability principle, so dear to the hearts of logical positivists, is simply not applicable here. Free will is not a matter of sense experience; it cannot be seen or felt. Neither can it be rationally demonstrated; one does not reach it as the conclusion of a syllogism. The act of choice is an intimate personal experience, the fact and nature of which can only be *intuited*.

Lest this admission cause scandal at the very outset of our enterprise, it should be realized that all knowledge depends ultimately upon intuition. Without intuitively known, self-evident propositions, the attempt to prove anything would be an interminable and futile process; one premise would have to be verified by another, that in its turn by a third, and so on endlessly. Indeed, in reasoning, even when the major and minor premises of the syllogism are accepted as true, one must still see that they prove the point, and this seeing is an intuition. The logical positivists themselves recognize, at least implicitly, the validity of intuition when, without bothering to prove it, they accept the verifiability principle as a perfectly obvious and fundamental truth.

Free will is so fundamental and obvious a fact of human experience that it is generally assumed: by parents when they punish their children for wrongdoing, by civil authorities when they jail and execute criminals, by anyone who praises or blames the actions of others. Even those philosophies which explicitly deny free will end up affirming it in one way or another. Stoicism, which held that God, as Reason immanent in the world, directs all things inexorably to certain fixed goals, left man a minimal area of freedom. He could recognize God's will in all that happened to him and in the world and either accept or resent it as he saw fit.

Spinoza's pantheism required him to reject free will as an a priori impossibility. Since finite beings were parts of God, their actions were necessary and determined. Men may think they are free, but this means nothing: a falling stone, if it were to become conscious, might also have the impression it was falling of its own accord. This would not free it from the law of gravity, however, and neither does man's ignorance of the factors dictating choice emancipate him from them.[1]

2

Yet in his *Ethics*, Spinoza expresses regret over the fact that the "road of salvation" is "so seldom found." It is not easy to find, he admits, but that does not account for its being "neglected practically by all." He wishes people would do something about it and strive to acquire a better nature.[2] A true and consistent determinist, one would think, should resignedly accept the fact that those foreordained to achieve salvation will inevitably do so and that the rest will not because they cannot.

David Hume also denied free will.[3] In his view, human conduct was as much caused as material actions were, as for example, the rebounding of a rubber ball. The regularity with which men of given dispositions acted in a constant and predictable way was for him evidence of a cause-effect relationship between character and action. Indeed, in his view, the only alternative to holding that human actions were caused was to attribute them to chance, in which case they would be mere random events for which neither God nor any human authority could hold the agent responsible. Hume wrote:

> According to my definitions, necessity makes an essential part of causation; and consequently liberty, by removing necessity, removes also causes, and is the very same thing with chance. As chance is commonly thought to imply a contradiction, and is at least directly contrary to reason, there are always the same arguments against liberty or free-will.[4]

Hume's doctrine on free will must be understood against the background of his theory of causality. He denied the traditional concept of cause—that which exerts a positive influence on the existence of something else, making it be—had any real value. For him the only objective element in causality was the constant conjunction of the so-called cause-and-effect. Every time one billiard ball strikes another, the one struck moves off. The mind imparts necessity to this observed sequence; by a psychological law it judges that what always happens has to happen; that, given this cause, this effect is inevitable.

3

Hume does well to preface his remarks on free will with the proviso "according to my definitions." Given his concept of causality, all he can mean when he says human action is caused is that it is, to a great extent at least, constant and predictable. This is true, of course, but it is not therefore unfree, for the possibility of its being self-caused or self-determined remains, and this is all that is required for freedom.

Inconclusive though we judge Hume's remarks on freedom to be, they have had great influence on subsequent philosophers, particularly the logical positivists. Moritz Schlick, founder of the Vienna Circle, felt that Hume had discussed the subject with such clarity and completeness that it had become a pseudoproblem, and he apologized for devoting a chapter to it in his *Problems of Ethics*.[5] With Hume, Schlick held that if choices are not caused, they are just chance events for which the agent is not responsible. He felt, too, that if ethics was to achieve what he considered its proper function, explaining human conduct, free choice could not be exempt from determinism; there had to be laws governing volition.

Schlick said that the will necessarily chooses the most pleasing, or the least displeasing, course of action proposed to it. He called this the "law of motivation," though he was unhappy that the word *law* should be used for a merely descriptive formulation or statement of fact such as this. It would be better, he thought, if only those enactments which require agents to act in a manner contrary to their natural inclination were called laws. His law of motivation was not a law in this sense. It no more compels the will to act as it does than the laws of celestial mechanics force the planets to move as they do rather than in some other way more to their liking. It was not prescriptive at all, but descriptive: it merely stated the way the will naturally and necessarily acts.

Schlick said that "the consciousness of freedom . . . is merely the knowledge of having acted of one's *own* desires."

These he defines as "those which have their origin in the regularity of one's character in the given situation, and are not imposed by an external power. . . ." For him, all that was needed for a person to be free was that he not be locked up, chained, or forced in some way, say at gunpoint, to do what he otherwise would not do; when, in other words, he is able to do what he wants to do. Schlick held this is all the freedom we are aware of and all that is needed for moral imputability. "I am responsible," he said, "not because my act was uncaused, but because it was the inevitable consequence of *my* desires."

For Schlick, motivation controlled conduct. Given a person's existing standard of values, the choice he makes on a given occasion is the only one he can make; and to say otherwise is to deny that he is the responsible author of his act. Other choices are compatible with the laws of volition, however, and if, on a later occasion, the person's motivation is changed, he will choose differently. This is why society punishes the thief whose motivation is all wrong, but not the kleptomaniac whose thefts are unmotivated. It made no difference to Schlick, either, whether the thief had gotten his antisocial tendencies from his parents or not. Since he had made them his own, they were to be dealt with as factors presently influencing him.

P. H. Nowell-Smith's concept of free will is similar to Schlick's.[6] Both assume a universal determinism which makes any uncaused act an impossibility. In his *Ethics*, Nowell-Smith analyzes the phrase "could have acted otherwise" and says it always connotes a contrary-to-fact condition: when a person says "I could have been a rich man," he means he is not rich but would have been if certain circumstances had not prevented him. Used in the context of morality, the phrase has this same meaning. When we say the thief could have acted otherwise, we mean he would have . . . if he had been differently motivated. He will continue to steal, predictably and inevitably, as long as he retains his larcenous attitude toward other people's property, but this does not exempt him from blame. He freely acquired this attitude and maintains it of his own accord. He should be punished, Nowell-Smith says, because he "could have acted otherwise." He did not, that is, *have* to have the mentality of a thief when the opportunity to steal presented itself. Hopefully, punishment will help him to revise his "pro-attitudes" so that his choices will be different in the future.

C. S. Campbell opposes both Schlick's and Nowell-Smith's concept of free will.[7] Universal determinism is for him an assumption which cannot stand against the common experience of free choice. The positivists' verifiability principle is inapplicable in this area, he holds; introspection is the only way of learning what free will is, and it reveals free acts as being contra-causal.

Campbell drastically restricts the area in which free will operates. In his view choice is possible only when duty and desire come into conflict. When the person sees no reason to do otherwise, he naturally and necessarily does what he pleases. His desiring nature takes over and determines the issue, so that the act is caused, determined, predictable. When duty and desire are in conflict, however, there is a break in causal continuity and the issue stands in doubt. The person must himself decide whether he will yield to desire or rise to duty. The choice he makes is an expression, not of his nature or character, but of his "Self"; it is unpredictable, uncaused, and therefore free. He is responsible for it because he could have acted otherwise. This phrase is for Campbell always categorical, never hypothetical, when used in a moral context. What the subject would have done . . . if he were some other person, or, being himself, were differently motivated, is for him beside the point. Unless, being what he was when he acted, he could have done otherwise, Campbell does not see how he can be in any way responsible for what he did.

6

To evaluate these profound insights into the nature of free will and choose among them is no easy task. Campbell does indeed seem to overrestrict the domain of human freedom. Though there is surely greater consciousness of freedom when duty and desire come into conflict, this hardly allows the conclusion that actions done out of natural inclination are not free. In fact, we appear to regard the predictability of such characteristic actions as an indication of freedom rather than an obstacle to it. How Winston Churchill would vote in a given election was never any great mystery, and yet he cast his vote freely, his political loyalties being, after all, of his own choosing. On the other hand, when a thief bent on robbing the poor box suddenly and inexplicably changes his mind, we are inclined to wonder what got into him and to regard him as more acted upon than acting of his own accord. As Nowell-Smith remarks, "To say that my choice depends on my character is not to say that my character compels me to do what I do, but to say that the choice was characteristic of me."

Defenders of the traditional concept of free will may feel that Nowell-Smith and Schlick prejudice to some extent the case for moral responsibility by overemphasizing the influence of character upon choice. They may prefer Campbell's concept of a transcendent "Self," uninfluenced by character, since this places freedom in the act itself rather than in the previous adoption of attitudes which make the act predictable and determined. It is not at all clear, however, that consciousness reveals the existence of any such "Self," aloof from the conflict of opposing interests and able to opt unpredictably in any direction. Introspection seems to reveal only that I am able to do what I want to do, so that even when I choose duty over desire, I do so because duty represents for the moment my dominant "pro-attitude." Nowell-Smith sums up the data which consciousness supplies on the subject rather well, we think, when he says that freedom means "to be free to do what one wants to do, not to be able to act in spite of one's desires."

The amount of determinism which Schlick and Nowell-Smith introduce into the free act is actually quite minimal; it is just enough to account for the general predictability of human behavior without destroying its freedom. As Nowell-Smith says, for a person's act to be free, it need not be *un*determined; it suffices that it be *self*-determined: "determined by his motives and character" and not "forced on him by circumstances or other people." And, though he holds that a person's "pro-attitudes" do indeed exert a casual influence over his choices, rendering them predictable, he saves freedom by making the person responsible for having acquired them in the first place and by leaving him always free to change them. No one, he says, ever becomes a "Pawn in the hands of Fate or a Prisoner in the iron grip of Necessity." This, we rather think, is sufficient safeguard for free will and moral responsibility.

I I

RESPONSIBILITY

Sartre holds that man is free in his every action. "Man cannot be at times free and at other times a slave: either he is always and entirely free or he is not free at all," he writes.[1] This is hardly true; there are areas in which man's acts come under compulsion. It is not choice but instinct that makes him quickly remove his hand from a hot stove or fling up his arm to ward off a blow directed at his head. These indeliberate acts, performed indeed by a human being, but without calling into play his specific faculties, intellect and will, are mere acts of man.

Only man's deliberate acts are free—those where good of some kind is seen to exist in the various alternatives without being overwhelming in any of them. Here choice is possible; one can seek good in the light of reason and act precisely as a man. Since, as Paul Tillich remarks, "Man is never more human than at the moment of decision,"[2] such choices are aptly termed human acts.

Since the will is the only free faculty man has, the only human act properly so-called is the choice or decision itself, the elicited act. In our everyday speech we attribute freedom to the commanded act, that done at the behest of the will, but this is inexact. When we say that we freely walk or talk, we attribute to the faculties or organs from which these acts proceed a perfection they do not in fact possess. Since the legs and tongue are not able to choose, it is not the walking or talking that is free, but only the decision to do so. This consideration led Kant to place the external act entirely outside the scope of morality; for him, only the will-act mattered. It seems more reasonable, however, to say that intention and execution form one moral unit and to include the commanded act in the material object or subject matter of ethics.

COMPONENTS OF THE HUMAN ACT

A human act has three components: knowledge, voluntariness, and freedom. There must be knowledge because what is unknown cannot be desired, intended, or willed. Voluntariness means that the will assumes an attitude, of desire or aversion, with regard to the known object. One might think there would be no further requirement; since the will is free, must not its every attitude be freely assumed? No, there are cases where the will acts under compulsion. The madman who, meat cleaver in hand, stalks his victim, knows what he is about and intends to kill, but is not responsible by reason of his dementia. For the act to be human, the intention or attitude must proceed from the will freely.

FACTORS WHICH MODIFY RESPONSIBILITY

Man is entirely responsible for such of his acts as are completely free and deliberate. Not all of them are, however, for man is not a pure spirit; he must operate in a world of space and time, subject to a great variety of stresses which interfere with his freedom. Modern techniques of human engineering are in fact so highly developed that he is often subtly influenced and manipulated without his even being aware of it. Psychologists know exactly what color factory walls should be painted and what kind of music piped in, so as to secure maximum productivity from the workers. Moralists, however, have traditionally considered that the factors affecting man's responsibility for his acts are reducible to five: ignorance, concupiscence, fear, force, and habit.

1 Ignorance is the lack of knowledge in a subject capable of it. It can render a person completely guiltless, even though what he did was objectively wrong. The will, as we have said, cannot tend toward an unknown object. The man who takes another's property, thinking it his own, does not commit theft in any formal sense. One who unjustly kills another, not recognizing him as his father, is guilty of murder but not parricide. When Oedipus married Jocasta, he did not incur the subjective guilt of incest because he did not know she was his mother.

Ignorance can be culpable, however, and when it is, one is responsible for any wrong done in virtue of it. Citizens are expected to know the law of the land and are justly punished when they violate it, even through ignorance. Professional men ought to know their field: a doctor is presumed to know medicine and is responsible for any harm that befalls his patient because of his ignorance of it. Not quite as guilty, to be sure, as if he had explicitly intended to injure him, but guilty nonetheless in that

11

he should have possessed the knowledge in question. He willed harm to his patient, not directly but indirectly, inasmuch as his deliberately maintained ignorance was its cause. We may say, then, that when ignorance is culpable, which it is when the knowledge is at hand and there is an obligation to possess it, guilt is diminished but not destroyed.

2 Concupiscence, or passion, as it is sometimes called, is a strong emotional response to stimulation. Such a reaction can arise without fault as when, in reading a novel which at first appears unobjectionable, one finds oneself in the midst of a lurid passage. The sexual desire thus innocently aroused might, on occasion, be so strong as to impel one to perform an objectively wrong action without being at all responsible for it.

Sudden anger can have the same effect and, recognizing this, courts of law distinguish between crimes of passion and those committed in cold blood. If it can be shown that the act was entirely unmotivated or indeliberate, the court will honor the defendant's plea of "temporary insanity." It will prudently decide that his desire—to kill, let us say—was irresistible, that something got into him, that he was not himself, that he could not have done otherwise.

Some psychologists believe this is what happens practically all the time. They see man as the helpless victim of subconscious forces and emotional drives which almost completely destroy his freedom. In their eyes the criminal, in particular, is a sick man, not to be punished but given medical and psychological treatment.

Their outlook on human behavior makes these psychologists oppose the M'Naghten Rule as a norm for determining criminal responsibility. This rule goes back to the trial of one Daniel M'Naghten in 1843. M'Naghten, a mentally disturbed person, was convinced that Sir Robert Peel was sending all sorts of spies and devils after him, and set out to kill him. By mistake he killed instead a Mr. Edward Drummond, Sir Robert's private secretary. Informed of Drummond's death, M'Naghten said it was "too bad," a comment which the prosecution later contended indicated he knew murder was wrong.

M'Naghten was acquitted, but the verdict so infuriated the nation that the presiding judges were required to justify it before the House of Lords. In answer to the Lords' questioning they formulated what has since been termed the M'Naghten Rule: that, even though a person be mentally ill, he is still criminally responsible if, when he committed the crime, he knew the nature and quality of the act, namely, that it was morally wrong.

Most American states still adhere to the M'Naghten Rule, but psychologists object that it looks only to the cognitive process and fails to view the individual as a whole. A disturbed person is simply not rational, they insist, and whether he knows the difference between right and wrong is really irrelevant. The courts have of late been showing an increasing tendency to agree with this more humane approach to responsibility. In 1954 the United States Court of Appeals, District of Columbia, overthrew the M'Naghten Rule in *Durham v. United States*, holding that "an accused is not criminally responsible if his unlawful act was the product of mental disease or mental defect." The psychiatrist-witness in the case was allowed to express his findings in medical rather than in merely legal or moral terms, and the jury was permitted to pass judgment on the accused person's responsibility as a separate issue from his de facto commission of the crime. In the Sirhan Sirhan case, the defense made the same distinction. It admitted that the accused had performed the mechanical act of pulling the trigger and killing Senator Robert Kennedy. It held, however, that he did so because of emotional or mental illness and therefore lacked the malice or specific intent required for full responsibility.

Some moralists side with the psychologists in delimiting the area of human freedom. Abbé Marc Oraison, for example, holds that most men incur no subjective guilt at all when they are unchaste. They are, he says, so completely dominated by the sexual drive that they are unable to resist performing impure actions and are, therefore, not answerable for them. The great majority of men have what he terms a "voluntary of choice," which means they can disapprove of what they have done, but no "voluntary of execution," since they cannot help doing it. In his opinion there is formal guilt only when the person approves of the evil he does and does not even wish he could control himself. His guilt lies, not in being sick, but in not desiring to get well.[3]

Even the most traditional among us will agree, in the light of all that has been discovered about the human psyche, that man is not quite as free as moralists have in the past considered him to be. Dipsomaniacs, kleptomaniacs and the like, lack control almost entirely in the area of their compulsion. Even the normal among us are unconsciously influenced by such factors as genetic origin, social and economic environment, parental taboos, and so forth. Nonetheless, freedom and responsibility are phenomena of which we are only too painfully aware. Though there are indeed occasions when desire is so strong that it sweeps reason aside and makes free choice impossible, this is not always or even usually the case. Normally, the person becomes aware that he is being tempted, that he can and should resist. He knows that, if he does so to the best of his ability—directing his thoughts into other channels, and so forth—he is not responsible for such evil desires as remain, or for what he does unintentionally under their influence. He realizes, too, that if he ignores the warning of conscience and dwells upon the evil proposed, he is responsible for the fascination it continues to have for him. If in the end he finds it so attractive that he cannot resist, he is all the more guilty for having ignored the warning of conscience at the outset.

Out of these considerations the principle emerges: when an objectively wrong action is done under the influence of antecedent concupiscence (desire which arises spontaneously and precedes the judgment of conscience), responsibility for it is decreased, perhaps entirely negated; when done under the influence of consequent concupiscence (that which is deliberately allowed to continue despite the warning of conscience), responsibility is increased.

3 Fear is the apprehension of impending evil. We do not here mean fright or hysteria, which are emotions and have already been treated under the heading of concupiscence. The fear we speak of is dispassionate and purely intellectual; the kind, for example, a bank employee experiences when, finding himself deeply in debt, he decides to become an embezzler. He acts under the influence of fear, choosing what appears to him the best way out of his predicament. He is responsible for his decision, of course, but somewhat less so than if he were not faced with the need to choose between two evils. We may say, then, that fear decreases guilt, but does not do away with it entirely.

St. Thomas makes the point that fear and passion affect the subject differently. Fear decreases both voluntariness and freedom while passion decreases freedom but increases voluntariness. The soldier who flees the battlefield because he fears death does not really want to do so. He is ashamed of his cowardice and wishes he had the courage to stand and fight; his action is, in a way, involuntary. A man inflamed by lust may lose control of himself, too, and be powerless to resist temptation, but there is this difference—his will embraces the evil proposed fervently and wholeheartedly, as if it were the supreme good. This analysis illustrates a point we have already made. Freedom and voluntariness are not identical, but separate and distinct qualities of the human act.

4 Force is external physical compulsion employed in order to make a person act against his will. We are not here speaking of the fear such aggression, or the threat of it, may engender, but only of the violence itself. Force is unique among

the factors which modify responsibility in that per se it does not effect the will, but only the body. If the victim of the assault does not consent internally to the wrong action, he incurs no guilt for what he is physically compelled to do. Not that one may simply submit to aggression on this ground. The victim of a rape attack would have to resist to the extent of her physical powers. Even if there were no hope that resistance would put an end to the attack, it would preclude or at least lessen the likelihood of internal consent.

5 Habit is an acquired disposition of mind or will which facilitates the performance of a given action. To become habitual, the action must be one which the subject performs freely. The heart beats all day long without our saying it is in the habit of beating, but the person who consistently rises early is said to do so habitually. Habits make the performance of the act easy and almost automatic. Since in so doing they improve upon nature, which merely makes the act possible of performance, they are called second nature.

As time goes on, we become increasingly creatures of habit, some good, others bad. We think of a good man as one who has good habits, and this is generally true. However, it is the person's total commitment, his character, that integrates his habits and ultimately determines their goodness. A thief can be patient, courageous, self-controlled, and temperate, but he is hardly a good man; he is in fact all the greater villain by reason of these virtues. As Kant remarked:

> Reasoning, wit, judgment, or whatever the *talents* of the intellect may be called, or such qualities of *temperament* as courage, determination and constancy of purpose, are doubtless good and desirable in many respects. But they may also be extremely evil and harmful unless the will be good which is to make use of these natural gifts and whose particular quality we therefore designate as *character*.[4]

16

Bad habits are to be avoided; if acquired, they must be broken. This means depriving them of what gave rise to them in the first place and presently sustains them—repetition of the given act. The person must determine not to repeat it deliberately and to avoid any occasion where he might do it indeliberately. If, despite these precautions, he fails in his resolution—blasphemes, let us say, in a fit of sudden anger—there is no guilt. Willed neither in itself nor in its cause, which would be the deliberately maintained bad habit, the blasphemy is not willed at all and is not a human act.

Getting rid of bad habits and acquiring good ones is often thought to involve will power, so that one who fails in his resolve is said to have a weak will. Our thought is that the power to will is equal in all men and that motivation is the deciding factor. No one, in the final analysis, ever does what he does not want to do; there is always some factor in the course of action he chooses that makes him regard it as the most desirable at the moment. Even when one "rises to duty" and resists his "desiring nature," as Campbell says, it is because duty exercises greater appeal at the time. Of two men who decide to give up smoking, the one who succeeds does so because of the good he sees in getting rid of the dirty habit, safeguarding his health, saving money, and so forth. The other fails because these benefits do not appeal to him strongly enough.

John Dewey saw the importance of motivation in breaking bad habits and forming good ones. He recommended making a game of it and concentrating on the good connected with the end rather than on the self-denial involved in the means. Alcoholics Anonymous recognizes, too, how easily frustration and boredom can defeat the determination of its members to pass up the next drink, and so its program requires frequent meetings at which their motivation is renewed. The Weight Watchers, one hears, try to inject a little fun into their grim reducing program. Taking the cue from their English members, they do not say "Good-bye" on parting, but "See you lighter!"

The need of making the acquisition of virtue an attractive and interesting process seems obvious enough. It conflicts, however, with the Kantian thesis that a human act has moral value only when it is done as a matter of grim duty. In Kant's view, a man who cares for his health purely as a matter of natural inclination, and not because he had an obligation to do so, does not perform a morally valuable act; though he acts dutifully, he does not act out of duty. If his desire to live were destroyed by adversity and grief, it would be different; his efforts to go on living would then have moral value because they would have duty as their motive, and duty for Kant was the essence and form of morality. The same was true of the philanthropist who gives away huge sums. If he does so because he likes to make other people happy, his generosity has no moral value. It would, however, if he were naturally cold and indifferent to the suffering of others and overcame this feeling as a matter of duty. Kant held that one should even seek happiness out of duty, because a consistently unhappy man is not likely to be responsive to moral obligation for very long.[5]

We do not find this Kantian thesis acceptable. While natural inclination is not a reliable guide to virtue, the fact that one finds the performance of duty pleasant does not deprive the act of its moral value. A married man's continence and faithfulness do not become morally worthless because he loves his wife and would find any violation of the marriage vows distasteful. The virtuous man is the human ideal, after all, and being virtuous means being so firmly committed to the good that we perform the good act easily and naturally. A man's actions should not have more moral value just because his soul is a battleground between virtue and vice.

Hegel saw this. Though he at first sided with Kant and thought of Christian morality in terms of grim duty, he came in time to regard it more as a matter of love and inspiration. He felt that for the true Christian there should be no opposition between law and life, no conflict between duty and inclination. Where Kant had held that the injunction "Love thy neighbor" required the Christian to perform only the external works of charity, on the grounds that the internal disposition could not be commanded, Hegel's view was that the Christian was supposed to become a new man, so that acts of charity would then be performed out of natural inclination, not as a matter of law.[6]

These reflections serve to show that, though man is indeed free, his freedom, and therefore his responsibility, is limited. As a composite of soul and body, he does not, except, perhaps, with his dying gasp, give himself over irretrievably to evil; there is always, in his embracing of it, an impermanent and tentative factor which makes withdrawal and forgiveness possible. This is not the case with pure spirits, St. Thomas tells us. Since their knowledge is not discursive but intuitive, it is impossible for them to alter a judgment once made or, since the will follows the intellect, any attitude of the will which is consequent upon an already formed judgment. This, he says, is why divine retribution followed immediately upon their sin, while redemption was granted to man after Adam's fall.[7]

THE MORAL LAW WITHIN

In our discussion of free will we made certain statements regarding its proper use. We said that the rape victim ought to resist, that a man should avoid evil and do good, that he will then be virtuous. We presupposed, in other words, that there is an objective moral law, that man is aware of his obligations under it, that he knows the difference between right and wrong.

CHALLENGE TO ETHICS

But is this true? Those intellectuals who, under the leadership of Moritz Schlick, formed the Vienna Circle in the 1920s denied it. They held that the concepts basic to morality—good

and bad, right and wrong, moral and immoral—mean nothing
at all. Ethics did not exist as a science because it had no subject
matter. Of their number, only Schlick concerned himself with
ethics. His view was that, though ethical terms as such meant
nothing, they could be made meaningful if they were reduced to
certain natural properties: if *good*, for example, were taken to
mean "desirable," "pleasurable," or "useful."[1] Ethical propositions could then be verified in terms of what an individual or
the community found to be of value.

For Schlick, nothing was inherently valuable; there was
nothing an individual or a community ought to hold dear, esteem, or prize. Value judgments were entirely subjective, matters of opinion. Ethics, therefore, could not be a normative
science. Its function was not to discover the way people ought to
behave, but only to find out what makes them think they must
live in the particular way they consider to be moral.

A. J. Ayer, a proponent of the emotivist theory, goes further than Schlick. For him, moral concepts are not only meaningless in themselves, they cannot be made meaningful. They
cannot be reduced to any natural quality, he holds, without committing what G. E. Moore quite properly termed the "naturalistic fallacy."[2] With Moore, Ayer holds that the term *good*, used
in the context of morality, simply does not mean what any given
person or community finds useful, pleasant, or desirable. One
can still ask: "Yes, but is it *good*?"[3]

In Ayer's view, nothing can be done to render moral concepts meaningful. Moore had tried to uphold objectivism by
appealing to intuition. We intuit the meaning of good and the
presence of moral obligation, he said. Ayer, however, distrusts
intuition. His objection is that what one man intuits, or says he
does, another cannot see at all, and there is no way of checking.
Moore had also used the fact that people argue about moral issues as proof that they find them objective and meaningful. Ayer
again disagrees. Such discussions, he says, never have to do with

the moral law itself because, its existence being unverifiable, it cannot be intelligently discussed. Arguments on ethical issues are therefore possible only between people who agree on a given moral code. Then the argument has to do only with the facts of the case—not with whether stealing is wrong, but whether, in the circumstances, the person can really be said to have stolen. One can verify whether one person took another's property, but not whether to do so is right or wrong.

Where Moore held that propositions having good as their predicate are always synthetic, never analytic, Ayer holds they are neither. They do not say what good is nor what is good. The term *good*, used in the context of morality, is for him a pseudoconcept, so that any statement in which it occurs is meaningless. And so of all moral terms. The only meaning he finds in the statement "You did wrong to steal" is "You stole," the statement being embellished with an exclamation mark or uttered in whatever tone of voice the speaker deems appropriate. For him, such statements are not even meaningful as disclosures of the speaker's own feelings or moral attitudes. To evince one's feelings, he says, is not the same as having them or even claiming to have them. One can cry "Ouch!" without being in pain or even, necessarily, asserting that one is. "Ouch!" says nothing, really, and neither do ethical propositions.

Ayer, then, does away with the subject matter of ethics and destroys it as an independent science. The only question left for it to deal with is: What moral habits has this person or this society adopted and why? This inquiry, he says, "falls within the scope of the existing social sciences." Casuistry, that part of ethics which deals with the application of moral principles to concrete situations, is for him just an exercise in logic.

IN DEFENSE OF ETHICS

This challenge to the very right of ethics to exist as an independent science must be met or our study of morality cannot even get under way. We must somehow determine whether the concepts basic to morality—good and evil, right and wrong, moral and immoral—are meaningful, whether moral value is objective, whether man is aware of the call to morality.

We say "somehow or other" but in fact there is no choice of method here. To discover whether moral concepts are meaningful, one can only consult one's own consciousness. If I understand them, then they mean something, at least to me. And indeed, looking within myself, I find these concepts quite meaningful. I can distinguish the moral aspect of my act, its rightness or wrongness, from all of its other qualities: the pleasure I got out of doing it, the cleverness I displayed in pulling the job off, the fact that I escaped detection, and so forth. The moral aspect could hardly be separable from the other aspects of the act if it were not intelligible in itself.

The authority of conscience does not have to be demonstrated to me, either. No one need prove to me that I must not answer "I will" when conscience says "Thou shalt not." I cannot seriously ask myself, "Why should I be moral?" any more than I can question why I should be logical or reasonable. The call to morality is intuited; I apprehend it in the depth of my consciousness. I find it addressed to me as a man. I am aware that I may in conscience refuse the opportunity to be good in other ways, a good doctor or lawyer, for example, but not the call to moral goodness. This takes precedence over all the others; it is the human vocation.

This, in brief, is what morality means to me. However, the fact that any single person finds moral value objective, the moral law absolute, and the call to morality of primary importance is not of world-shaking importance. Ayer would consider it of "purely psychological interest," and Schlick would view it as something to be "explained." It is necessary, then, to ascertain whether my personal conviction in this area is an individual idiosyncrasy or is shared by mankind as a whole.

The latter is quite evidently the case. People are generally aware of the meaning of morality and its importance in human affairs. For no other reason than the presence or absence of moral goodness do they label a man "good" or "bad" simply and without qualification. When an act is conspicuously heroic or beneficent, they have medals struck or statues erected in the public square to show their approval of it. On the other hand, the whole world condemned the Nazi attempt at genocide: not for being bad manners, poor public policy, or contrary to the Geneva Convention, but as morally wrong. The vast generality, it seems evident, knows what right and wrong mean, realize that one must do the one and avoid the other, and have standards for judging the rectitude of human conduct.

The high esteem people have for moral idealism is utilized, sometimes exploited, by their political leaders. When they are called to war, it is never for any such pedestrian reason as economic advantage or mere military necessity. The Crusaders went to liberate the Holy Land because "God wills it"; the French Revolutionaries fought in the name of "liberty, fraternity, equality"; the doughboys of World War I were supposed to "Make the world safe for democracy." The English people achieved their "finest hour" largely because Churchill rang the changes so eloquently on the moral rightness of their cause as opposed to the tyranny and treachery of the enemy. Moral idealism, it would appear from the power of such appeals to it, speaks quite forcefully to the human heart.

Literature, always an index of what people find meaningful and important, offers further confirmation of our thesis. From the ancient sagas down to the modern "westerns," the confrontation between good and evil is an ever-recurring theme. No other subject, it seems, so readily enlists the sympathy of the reader. He loathes the villain and identifies himself with the hero, the man of virtue, whose function is to right all wrongs and make justice triumph. William Faulkner knew this; he once

24

said that a novelist should leave "no room in his workshop for anything but the old verities and truths of the heart, the old universal truths, lacking which, any story is ephemeral and doomed —love and honor and pity and pride, compassion and sacrifice."[4] Coleridge's encomium on Shakespeare also comes to mind in this connection:

> . . . he never renders that amiable which religion and reason alike teach us to detest, or clothes impurity in the garb of virtue . . . he does not use a faulty thing for a faulty purpose, nor carries on warfare against virtue, by causing wickedness to appear as no wickedness, through the medium of a morbid sympathy with the unfortunate. In Shakespeare, vice never walks as in twilight . . .

People generally are aware of the nature of morality and the kind of obligation the moral law imposes. They do not blame a man for falling when he loses his balance, even though he happens to break the china. They fully realize a physical law is at work here, that the subject is not free. They readily distinguish moral obligation from psychological compulsion, too. However impatient they may be with the neurotic who feels he must check over and over again to make sure he has not left any cigarettes burning before he can bring himself to leave the house, they do not condemn his action as immoral. They distinguish, too, between guilt itself and subsequent feelings of guilt—Lady Macbeth's wrongdoing in having Duncan killed, for example, and the torment of conscience she went through later on.

The great philosophers of the past had none of the difficulty Schlick and Ayer profess to find in understanding moral concepts or in adopting an intellectualist approach to ethics. For Socrates, knowledge and virtue were one and the same. The wise man was the good man; to know one's true good was to seek it; no one pursued evil knowingly and willingly, and so there was always an element of ignorance or deception in wrongdoing.

Informed by the Delphic Oracle that he was the wisest man alive, Socrates spent his lifetime inducing his fellow Athenians to take care of their souls by acquiring wisdom and virtue. He would engage them in conversation, speaking at random until some ethical term was used—piety, perhaps, or justice or courage. Making use of a stratagem we now call Socratic irony, he would profess ignorance of its meaning. A tentative definition being given, he would praise it to the skies, but always manage to find certain minor faults with it: this act, clearly unjust, would fall under the concept of justice so defined, while this other, clearly just, would not. Gradually, through trial and error, the dialectic would make its way toward a more or less acceptable definition of the given virtue. The entire process was aimed at action. Once a satisfactory definition was attained, it was supposed to act as a moving principle in the person's mind; knowing the nature of justice would make him forever just. Morality was for Socrates, as indeed for the ancient Greeks generally, a matter of aesthetics, rather than of duty or law, but before a virtue could exert its appeal upon the person, its inherent goodness had to be known.

Plato accepted Socrates' identification of virtue and knowledge. He made prudence queen of the virtues. The prudent man sought his true good in every area and was therefore just, pious, courageous, temperate, and so forth. The human soul, he held, was tripartite. Only the rational part was spiritual and immortal; the spirited and appetitive parts were material and would perish. The rational part of the soul was the charioteer, whose function it was to drive the two horses committed to him, giving full rein to the spirited one because of its love of honor, but restraining the appetitive one with a strong and heavy whip because of its depravity.[5]

If, on occasion, the bad horse went his own way, it was because the charioteer either did not know the true good or, knowing it, culpably allowed this knowledge to be obscured by passion. But, as for Socrates so also for Plato, the object of choice was always the good, either true or merely apparent. The key to the good life was knowledge of the true good; such knowledge, when deep and abiding, made one proof against all temptation; such knowledge was virtue. And a man could know his true good. There was nothing subjective or relative about it; it was objective and immutable. The *good* was in fact the highest of the forms, the perfect object of *episteme*, the purest kind of knowledge. In its full transcendence it was apprehended only by philosophers, which was why only they should be kings. For the lesser occupations partial knowledge will do; it is enough if the farmer knows only husbandry. But the state must minister to the total needs of men, and so whoever rules it must know the *good* as such.

Aristotle criticized Socrates' moral theory for being over-intellectualist and not taking moral weakness into consideration. The "irrational parts of the soul" could, he felt, so overwhelm reason as to make a man perform an objectively wrong act without it seeming wrong at all to him. But for Aristotle too, the intellectual virtue of prudence was man's guide. It moderated his feelings and actions, keeping them always "in the middle," so that they deviated from the norm neither by deficiency nor excess. It prevented the courageous man from being either reckless or cowardly, the generous man from being either prodigal or stingy. Aristotle defined moral virtue as "a disposition to choose, consisting essentially in a mean relatively to us determined by a rule, that is, the rule by which a practically wise man would determine it."[6] Morality for him, as for Socrates and Plato, clearly had an intellectual content.

Many modern philosophers have been as aware of the meaningfulness of morality and its primacy in human affairs as these ancients. Kant made the moral law the law of reason. Obedience to it was the supreme purpose of a rational being's existence. "It is impossible," he wrote, "to conceive of anything in

27

this world, or indeed out of it, which can be called good without qualification save only a good will"[7]—and the will became "good" by observing to the full the categorical imperatives laid down by practical reason.

Fichte found reality intelligible only in terms of morality; the world was real to him only as the sphere of moral rights and duties.[8] Answering the call to morality was, he felt, his "true vocation, the whole end and purpose" of his life, taking priority over all other relationships and giving meaning to them. This he considered true, not only for himself, but for everyone; it applied "even to one who had never meditated on his own moral vocation, if there could be such a one, or who, if he had given it some general consideration, had never had any intention of fulfilling it at any definite time in the future." Such a person may not apprehend the sensuous world by the thought of his duties, but he certainly does so by the demand for his rights:

> [W]hat he may never require of himself, he certainly exacts of others in their conduct toward him—that they should treat him with propriety, consideration, and respect, not as an irrational thing, but as a free and independent being. . . . Even should he never propose to himself any other purpose in his use and enjoyment of surrounding objects but simply that of enjoying them, he at least demands this enjoyment as a right in the possession of which he claims to be left undisturbed by others; and thus he apprehends even the irrational world of sense by means of a moral idea.

This great weight of evidence, drawn from personal consciousness and supported by the testimony of mankind generally, requires the conclusion that the concepts basic to morality are meaningful, that there is a moral law, that man's call to morality is absolute and of primary importance.

VARIOUS PROPOSED NORMS

OF MORALITY

The concepts basic to morality—good-evil, right-wrong, moral-immoral—are meaningful, then, and the injunction "Do good, avoid evil," which every man finds addressed to him through conscience, is the first and most basic law of human nature. But how does conscience arrive at its decisions on what is good and to-be-done, evil and to-be-avoided? What makes respect for human life right, murder wrong? What, in other words, is the norm or standard of moral value?

THE POINT AT ISSUE

Philosophers have answered this question in a great variety of ways, and we shall evaluate them. Needless to say, we shall not give serious consideration to any theory that denies the existence of the moral law, the reality of man's call to morality, or the primacy of the moral issue in human affairs. We have already established all this, and theories are supposed to explain facts, not question them.

HEDONISM

We dismiss hedonism on this ground. Aristippus' teaching that sense gratification is the purpose of human life in effect does away with the moral law altogether. If there is no need ever to curb our passions and desires, then there is no ought for morality to concern itself with.

EPICUREANISM

The refinements which Epicurus introduced into the basic Cyrenaic doctrine that pleasure is the end of life keep his doctrine from being, as so often popularly depicted, a philosophy of complete debauchery. He placed the joys of the spirit above those of the body and counseled against the active and immoderate pursuit of pleasure because this was more likely to stimulate desire than satisfy it. The happy man in his view was the one who had achieved ataraxy, the absence of desire—a state of mind not far removed from the Stoic ideal of apathy or unconcern. A faithful Epicurean might in fact find himself stoically enduring considerable privation and self-denial, though not for the very best of motives.

Lucretius tells us that Epicurus wanted only to show people how to be happy. If so, he did a fairly good job. The Epicurean gods were so pleasant and attractive that it would take a very timorous person indeed to fear them. Their beautiful bodies, he said, were constructed of atoms even more finely textured than those composing the human soul. They dwelt in intermundia, eternally banqueting and happily conversing—in Greek, to be sure!—with never a thought of this sad world of ours. One need not be worried about falling into their hands, therefore, either in this life or the next. In fact, there was no future life; as a materialist, Epicurus taught that death meant annihilation.

CRITIQUE

Epicurus' good intentions do not ensure the soundness of his moral theory, however. Pleasure is meaningful to man, but it is not his sole concern or his primary good. As Romanell remarks, man has not just a "eudaemonistic," but also a "juristic" side; he is not only a "producer and consumer of happiness," but also a "maker and keeper of obligations."[1] Epicurus ignores this aspect of man, in fact misses the moral point of view altogether. When he says, for example, that "Injustice is not intrinsically bad; it has this character only because there is joined with it a fear of not escaping those who are appointed to punish actions marked with that character,"[2] he confuses the moral aspect of injustice with the separate and distinct question of punishment. Since Epicurus had no clear idea of what morality is, we can hardly expect from him any valid theory on the norm of moral value.

UTILITARIANISM AND ALTRUISM

If human acts are not morally good simply because they afford the agent pleasure, then perhaps the beneficial effect they have on others plays a part in the determination of their moral value. This is what Bentham held. Though for him pleasure was the end of life and the individual was psychologically necessitated to seek it, he recognized that happiness was possible only in a well-ordered society. He counseled, therefore, that the moral arithmetic needed to determine the happiness-producing qualities of the contemplated act should take into account the community as a whole. As a materialist, Bentham saw no essential difference between man and beast, and would have animals included in the computation. One's aim, he held, should be to promote the "greatest happiness of the greatest number."[3]

Though Bentham's moral theory took cognizance of man's social nature, it was essentially individualistic; one did good to others in order to benefit oneself. Comte, however, would have the individual forget himself entirely and "live for others." The truly good man for him was one who had learned to subordinate his own welfare to the common good: that of the family, the state, and above all, humanity which he considered a goddess worthy of worship.[4]

John Stuart Mill followed Comte in attributing moral value only to acts which promote the social good. In his view the individual should be a "disinterested spectator" where his own or other people's private good is concerned.[5] More recently, W. T. Stace has held that, to have moral value, an act must be altruistic. His reason is that, if acts done out of the natural inclination to benefit oneself had moral value, one would never have any reason to deny oneself for the sake of others.[6]

CRITIQUE

Bentham and Comte rightly reject a hedonism which sees moral value only in acts which promote one's own personal pleasure. They are right, too, in ascribing more moral value to acts which benefit the neighbor than to those which serve only one's own interests. We take exception only to the thesis, more Comte's than Bentham's, that an act which benefits oneself alone has no moral value.

The person who takes proper care of his health, defends himself against a mugging attack, or goes on strike for a fair wage may well have no intention of doing good to anyone but himself, but this hardly deprives his act of moral value. Psychologists in fact tell us that one who does not love himself cannot really love anyone else. This means that love of self, or self-esteem, as it is better called, is the psychological foundation of the whole moral order, which makes it difficult to see why acts prompted by it should automatically lack moral value.

The firmness with which man has been steered in the direction of his proper good by his natural inclinations appears to need some emphasis in our day. One thinks of those misguided young people who set themselves afire in protest against our country's involvement in Vietnam. They were, apparently, unaware of the moral directive imposed upon them by the instinct of self-preservation. Surely there were many others, equally opposed to the war, who found this form of protest repugnant to their natural and well-ordered love of self. Can it be said that their rejection of it on this ground lacked moral value?

Not only can an act by which one seeks one's own good have moral value; an act by which one intends to benefit another may very well lack it. Those nice old ladies in *Arsenic and Old Lace* come to mind in this connection. They had the purest charity in their hearts when they poisoned their boarders' wine: they wanted only to get them out of this vale of tears as painlessly as possible. One would prefer to be spared such altruism, however.

Even when the act truly benefits another, it can still be wrong, if viewed in its total context. Dr. Samuel Mudd surely did John Wilkes Booth a good turn when he set his broken leg. In doing so, however, he made it possible for President Abraham Lincoln's assassin to escape. The federal authorities, taking the larger view, considered he had done wrong and sentenced him to life imprisonment.

The principle which the federal government invoked against Dr. Mudd, that the good of the community takes precedence over that of any private person, is a valid one. It does not mean, though, that just because the act is done in the service of the community it automatically has moral value. Whether Hitler could have produced a better Germany through elimination of the Jews is really beside the point. No goal, however desirable, sanctions murder. Even an act meant to benefit the entire race, and perhaps actually doing so in a materialistic sort of way, such as sterilizing every other male child in order to curtail the population explosion, can lack moral goodness. It seems clear, therefore, that altruism, even when carried to the highest level, is not the norm of morality. There is need for a broader and more comprehensive standard which will tell us when we may in conscience procure this good for this neighbor or community at this time.

MORAL POSITIVISM

The question whether moral value is absolute, necessary, and in the very nature of things or merely the result of historical accident was first raised by the ancient Greeks. While they lived in the isolation of their city-states, they took it for granted that their way of life was the properly human one. As they came increasingly into contact with foreigners who worshiped different gods and did not even speak Greek, the disquieting question occurred: Could Hellenic culture be merely an accident of history, owing more to custom than to nature?

Callicles the sophist and Carneades the skeptic opted for custom, holding that moral right and wrong was purely a matter of the life-style adopted by a given community. Plato put their view in the mouth of Protagoras, he of "Man is the measure of all things" fame:

> For I hold that whatever practices seem right and laudable to any particular State are so for that State, so long as it holds by them.[7]

This is the view of moral positivism, the best-known proponent of which was Thomas Hobbes.[8] For him, morality had its practical origin in civil law. In what he called the "state of nature," which is to say, the human condition prior to—or, more

34

properly, without—the state, he held that "the notions of right and wrong, justice and injustice, have no place. Where there is no common power, there is no law, where no law, no injustice . . . no dominion, no *mine* and *thine* distinct; but only that to be every man's that he can get; and for so long as he can keep it." "The desires and other passions of man are in themselves no sin," he said. "No more are the actions that proceed from those passions till they know a law that forbids them, which till laws be made, they cannot know, nor can any law be made till they have agreed upon the person that shall make it." In the meantime, life was "solitary, poor, nasty, brutish, and short," a "war of all against all," with every man a "wolf" to his neighbor. Ethics, which Hobbes defined as the "science of those things which are good or evil in the congresses and societies of men," had no place in this period; its subject matter did not exist.

Hobbes held that contracts made prior to the political covenant were just "empty words," because the parties to them were in the "condition of war" and would quite understandably fear nonfulfillment. But once the state is formed, contracts become valid and binding, because the state's coercive power actuates the third "law of nature" which requires that "Men perform their covenants made."

Hobbes' purpose in writing on politics and morals was to bring peace to his native land. He had just seen England emerge from the disastrous Civil War, in the course of which its people had considered only themselves and shown precious little concern for the general welfare. Hobbes generalized upon this experience and concluded that man was inherently antisocial. Inevitably then, as a society of men, the state had within it disruptive forces and stood desperately in need of a counterforce powerful enough to hold it together. This, he felt, could be supplied only by an all-powerful sovereign. The diffusion of political authority in the past had, in his opinion, occasioned the recent Civil War:

If there had not been an opinion received of the greater part of England, that these Powers (of legislative, administering justice, raising taxes, controlling doctrines and so on) were divided between the King and the Lords and the House of Commons, the people had never been divided and fallen into this Civil War.

In order to make rebellion theoretically impossible in the future, Hobbes made the sovereign the ultimate source of all law, all morality, all rights. He could not violate the political covenant because he was not a party to it; it was a compact made by the people and binding only upon them. The sovereign's authority was absolute; he could do no wrong: "Whatsoever he doth, it can be no injury to any of his subjects; nor ought he to be by any of them accused of injustice."

CRITIQUE

Hobbes' concept of man as being inherently antisocial is not borne out by experience. Quite the contrary; people have an instinctive love and concern for one another. When a child is trapped in a well or miners in a cave, the resources of the entire nation are placed at their disposal. When it was feared that the Apollo XII astronauts might be unable to return to earth, the whole world felt for them. The Scholastic thesis that man is by nature social, so that political society is based on friendship and the desire to cooperate, comes closer to the truth than Hobbes' attempt to found it on hostility and distrust. St. Thomas writes:

It is natural for all men to love one another; a sign of this is that, by a certain natural instinct, a man helps any man, even a stranger, in necessity, as by recalling him from a wrong turn in the road, raising him up after a fall, and in other matters of this kind, as if every man were to every other a relative and friend.[9]

Hobbes errs, too, when he raises peace and public order to the status of absolutes. Desirable as these are, there are justifying causes for civil disobedience and even revolution. Sovereigns are only human, after all, and may easily be in the wrong. Hobbes affords the citizen no effective remedy for this contingency. Though he speaks of the "natural law" and calls it a "dictate of reason," the fact remains that only the sovereign can authoritatively determine what it prescribes. Hobbes says the sovereign is responsible to God and will suffer divine retribution if he does not govern in the public interest, but this is cold comfort for the citizen who in the meantime is unjustly treated and can do nothing about it.

On analysis, then, Hobbes' moral theory proves to be merely a canonization of the principle that "Might makes right." The subject is to obey for no other reason than that he will otherwise be punished; his acts have moral value only when he abjectly and without question submits to the sovereign will. Actually, man's dignity lies chiefly in his power of self-direction and he is never justified in surrendering it to a fellow mortal so completely as to obey him without question. This point, obvious in itself, was made at the Nuremberg Trials where it was held that subordinates must not obey when ordered to do what is wrong. There must, then, be a higher norm of moral value than mere obedience to the sovereign will, one which tells us when it is right to obey.

LIBERTY AS THE NORM

If a human act is not morally good precisely because it is done in obedience to the will of another, then perhaps its moral value derives from its being an uninhibited expression of the Self. Perhaps human acts are good when they are completely free, evil when there is any yielding to pressure or compulsion.

This is what existentialism holds. The proponents of this rather disorganized philosophy differ widely among themselves, but have one theme in common: the inherent value of the human person and the ideal of self-expression. They draw much of their inspiration from Kierkegaard's reaction against the Hegelian subordination of the individual to the universal, of man to the system. Man was not, Kierkegaard contended, a mere puppet in the hands of an unfeeling nature pursuing ends of its own according to the relentless dictates of any dialectic. Rather, he was an independent Self, a center of responsibility.

For Kierkegaard it was man as an individual, not as a species or a universal, that mattered and indeed alone was real. The important thing was how people differed from one another, not what they had in common. For this reason abstract thinking had its limitations. It was applicable to science where the concern is with the essence of the thing, not its particularity. But it was no help in discerning ethical or moral truth. There the approach had to be personal; it was the subject that mattered, not the object, and one had to guard against the temptation to become a mere mind, abstracting the human individual from his concrete setting. There the proper method was introspection; it was the only way a person could get to know himself and insure against the greatest peril he faces—the loss of his identity:

> For a self is the thing the world is least apt to inquire about, and the thing of all things the most dangerous for a man to let people notice he has. The greatest danger, that of losing one's self, may pass off as quietly as if it were nothing; every other loss, that of an arm, a leg, five dollars, a wife, etc. is sure to be noticed.[10]

Kierkegaard also challenged Hegel's doctrine on the gradual rationalization of nature, its continuous conquest by the Idea. He himself found reality for the most part absurd and unintelligible. Man was not saved by ideas or membership in a church, but by faith. And faith for Kierkegaard was a trusting leap in the dark without any rational justification whatsoever.

For him, Abraham was the archtype of the religious man. Casting reason and the moral law aside, he was ready at God's command to slay his son Isaac. He was no murderer, though; it was a case of the "suspension of the ethical." Though the moral law prohibiting killing of the innocent remained in force for the generality of men, God suspended it in this instance in order to

38

elicit from Abraham an act of faith. The incident established to Kierkegaard's satisfaction the superiority of the religious over the moral and of the individual over the generality.

Kierkegaard was not much read in his time. He wrote in Danish, which is not exactly a lingua franca, and besides, his attacks on the established Lutheran Church, of which he was a minister, did not endear him to his countrymen. His opposition to Hegelian rationalism and his esteem for the human person suited the post-World War II mood, however, and his ideas caught on. The war had been so obvious a regression to irrationalism and barbarism that it was difficult to believe any longer in the inevitable conquest of nature by the Idea. People had been killed, both on the battlefield and in concentration camps, with such callous indifference that the worth of the human individual badly needed to be reaffirmed.

Existentialism reaffirmed it in no uncertain terms, and by 1946 it was all the vogue in Europe. Its adherents were not just intellectuals; on the contrary, some of the *existentialistes* who met with Sartre in the boulevard cafés along St. Germain des Prés could hardly read or write. In the beginning, *existentialisme* was so closely associated in the popular mind with jazz, night clubs, and youthful rebellion that Heidegger disclaimed any association with the movement. Sartre has no such inhibitions. He, the high priest of the existentialist movement, once said he had spent his whole life in cafés and could not work anywhere else. He so unreservedly makes the claim that liberty is the norm of moral law, the point at issue here, that we shall limit our discussion to what he has to say on the subject.

Sartre divides reality into the *in-itself* and the *for-itself*. Sense experience reveals the in-itself: it has no power of choice and is full of being, without potentiality for further perfection; it just *is*. Any attempt to explain its existence would mean postulating causes outside itself and, ultimately, the existence of God. God, however, as traditionally conceived, is a being at once simple and yet both for-himself and in-himself. Since this involves a contradiction, God for Sartre is an "impossible."

Sartre viewed man as a complex being, partly in-himself, since he has a body and certain fixed habits, partly for-himself, since he is free. Insofar as he is free, he is nothing; he *is*, but he is not tied down to any particular mode of being. He can choose what he pleases and can therefore be what he pleases. He is his choice and is therefore always in transit, never being, always becoming. He is a choice in the process of being made and he inherits nothing from the past, either from himself or others. Sartre put his concept of freedom in the words of Mathieu: "Within me there is nothing, not even a wisp of smoke; there is no within. There is nothing. I am nothing. I am free. . . ."[11]

Sartre, as we have said, felt that any attempt to explain the existence of being-in-itself by means of causes outside itself would ultimately require admitting God's existence as unproduced First Cause. He found the same difficulty in allowing the moral value of an act to be determined by a standard outside itself. If this were done, then the process could ultimately be terminated only in an absolute standard which would have to be an Absolute Being, God. To avoid this—and alternatively a *processus in infinitum*, which offended his rigidly logical mind—he refused to go outside the act itself to find the source of its goodness. It had moral value simply because it was free. Man, he held, created moral value simply by choosing. There were no objective norms to guide him. Sartre wrote:

> My freedom is the unique foundation of values. And since I am the being by virtue of whom values exist, nothing—absolutely nothing—can justify me in adopting this or that value or scale of values. As the unique basis of the existence of values, I am totally unjustifiable. And my freedom is in anguish at finding that is is the baseless basis of values.[12]

Thus, for Sartre, no choice is inherently better than another. The habitual drunkard who—because his wife is ill, say

—decides to omit his usual visit to the saloon and return home with his salary intact affirms new values: sobriety, self-respect, love. There is no assurance that he will continue to affirm them, nor is he under any obligation to do so; this would be an interference with his freedom, which by definition is uninhibited, untrammeled, absolute. Neither is his present role as a faithful husband any nobler, really, than his former one as an immoderate drinker, and when he ceases to affirm the new values they will cease to exist.

CRITIQUE

We shall base our estimate of Sartre's moral theory for the most part on what Gabriel Marcel has said of it.[13] His view is balanced, for, though himself an existentialist with profound respect for Sartre's genius, calling him a man of "prodigious intelligence," he is nevertheless somewhat fearful that Sartre's tone of rebellion and bohemianism may seduce the uncritical minds of the young.

Marcel calls Sartreism "in the last analysis, a philosophy of non-being" because it sees no good in anything. Sartre speaks of the "nausea" he experiences when he contemplates the contingency and absurdity which characterizes existence as such. What exists does so "to the point of swelling, of mouldering, of obscenity." Human beings in particular are obscene, "embarrassed by their existence," feeling absurd as they chew the "insipid cud of [their] thoughts." Dead or alive, celibate or with their "gaggle of brats," it makes no difference; they are "superfluous to all eternity." Freedom, which distinguishes man from what is merely in-itself and makes him uniquely for-himself, is not, for Sartre, a perfection, but something forced upon him. Man is "condemned" to be free; freedom is not an attribute of man or a power he uses; it is man himself, his very being or, as Sartre would have it, the lack of it, the reason he is nothing.

41

Since for Sartre "freedom is the unique foundation of values," there is no such thing as a wrong use of freedom. Marcel wonders whether he "does not here go counter to the exigencies of that human reality which he claims, after all, not to invent but to reveal." Marcel's point is that moral value is discovered by the individual and not constituted by his choice. This is indeed the case. Consciousness discloses that it is *I* who am devaluated when I reject what is objectively of value, that honesty and truth-telling are not affected by my becoming a thief or liar but remain as norms despite any action of mine.

Marcel notes that Sartre is not entirely consistent in his denial of objective norms governing choice. Sartre announced, prior to the publication of his *Les Chemins de la Liberté*, that he would dedicate it to the men of the Resistance. Marcel asks on what grounds, if there is no objective norm to which choice must conform, Sartre holds these in higher esteem than those equally brave men who joined the Anti-Bolshevik Legion. It cannot be on the basis of choice alone, for both groups chose the side they preferred. It can only be because the heroes of the Resistance chose what was truly of value, the choice of the others being misguided. Sartre appears to affirm here implicitly what he professedly denies: that there are norms governing the rightness or wrongness of choice.

Marcel points out another contradiction between Sartre's theory and practice, this time in his attitude toward reason. Sartre says he distrusts reason. When he comes to God, he ought, then, to merely will Him out of existence, on the ground that he simply does not like Him or for some other nonreason. This might be somewhat absurd, but it would at least be consistent with his basic position. Instead, he attempts to prove the point. Since certain organisms have failed to adapt to change, he says, there is a lack of purposefulness in the universe which indicates the nonexistence of God. Marcel quite properly chides Sartre

42

for appealing to reason in order to lay the foundation for a philosophy which professes to reject reason.

Marcel also notes that Sartre frequently uses the words *good* and *bad* in the context of choice and asks what he can possibly mean by them. They seem to imply the existence of a norm outside the choice itself which determines its value. Sartre also recommends "commitment" and "engagement" as the proper way of life, making one wonder whether those who prefer to lose themselves in the crowd and who refuse to get involved do wrong by failing to live up to the norm he proposes. If so, it sounds very much like the old moral law in another guise. *Authenticity* is another one of his favorite words, and he in fact defines it in terms of old-fashioned and easily recognizable virtues: as a "kind of honesty or a kind of courage." This again indicates that it is not the choosing itself that has value, but the properly directed choice.

Then too, Sartre's denial of essence raises philosophical problems. The terms he uses—*good, bad, honesty, courage,* and so forth—must have meaning; they must designate some objective reality or else they are just words, in which case Sartre's entire philosophy becomes a mere nominalism. This is particularly the case with the word *freedom*, which is the norm for his distinction between the in-itself and the for-itself. If this distinction is not wholly mental, there must be some objective basis for it. The for-itself must possess some mode of being by virtue of which it is free, but which is lacking in the in-itself, so that it is determined in its activity. This mode of being, which makes it possible for things to be and yet to be different, Scholastics call essence.

Sartre's faulty metaphysics accounts in large part for the errors in his moral theory. His denial of nature or essence allows him to avoid the problem of a moral law based upon the individual's obligation to act in accordance with what he is, to make his behavior conform to the reality he represents, so that being a man involves acting like one. The objective validity of the concept of nature or essence is not that easily set aside, however, nor is the general conviction that there is a norm which determines when liberty is rightly used. For these reasons we must reject Sartre's moral theory.

PRESSURE AS THE NORM

Some see morality as resulting from pressure of one kind or another—the weak against the strong, the fit against the unfit, the haves against the have-nots. For them there is nothing necessary or absolute about the moral law; as the product of social, economic, or evolutionary forces, it is subject to constant change.

Nietzsche, for example, attributed the present ascendancy of the Judaeo-Christian moral code to the pressure exerted by the more numerous weak peoples upon the strong. It all began with the Jews, whom nature had made an inferior race. In order to avoid being enslaved by their more generously endowed neighbors, they invented a moral law according to which it was wrong to employ cunning, ruthlessness, and superior strength in order to gain ascendancy over others. The Christians adopted this slave morality and incorporated it into the law of Christ. For Nietzsche, however, there was nothing valid or objectively binding about it. It was a human invention, as indeed were the very notions of good and evil. He thought of reality in terms of the Dionysian-Apollonian antithesis. Dionysus represented the power of life, unrestrained and boundless, while Apollo stood for clarity and intelligibility, restraint and order. The two, acting in concert and in proper balance, ensured aesthetic productivity. The arbitrariness of the Church, for example, honed and sharpened the European spirit and produced a first-class civilization. Of the two principles, however, Nietzsche favored the Dionysian, because what really counts is life; the world is Dionysian, he held, and this puts it "beyond good and evil."

44

Nietzsche would have the "Superman" become fully conscious of his identification with the Dionysian principle, realize that "life is precisely the Will to Power,"[14] and that "the Superman is the meaning of the earth."[15] As nature's appointed agent he should fulfill her purpose: subject the inferior peoples of the earth to himself and establish master morality, which alone has value for him.

For Herbert Spencer the pressure exerted by evolutionary forces gave rise to the moral law. Man, who is without free will, naturally adopts those ways of doing things which he finds useful. The practice in time becomes customary and finally obligatory. Thus the moral law develops, always in harmony with the existing stage of man's evolution.

Spencer saw in man, not just egoistic and hedonist tendencies, but also an inclination toward altruism. This would grow ever stronger, he thought, and motivate human action more and more as the evolutionary process went on. Inevitably, therefore, complete or absolute morality would one day come to be, and people would then do the right, which is to say the unselfish, thing naturally and instinctively. He wrote:

> The actions to which men are today subject with repugnance because they are presented as obligatory will be accomplished without effort and with pleasure; in addition, those which man now avoids by a feeling of duty, he will then avoid, because they are disagreeable to him.[16]

Spencer felt that the human race had already made remarkable progress toward its final goal—it had evolved all the way from its animal beginnings to the drawing rooms of Victorian England! There was still a long way to go, of course, but nature was busily at work and would inevitably succeed in producing a perfect race of men, fully adapted to their environment. Her principal task—in accomplishing which she needed no help from God, parents, or public authorities—was strengthening the moral institutions of the Elect, seeing to it that they found ever more joy in doing good. Altruism, Spencer held, gave moral value to human acts, and was the quality nature looked for in those destined for survival.

Karl Marx also held that the ideal man and absolute morality would inevitably come to be, but for him the pressure exerted upon the moral law had its source in economic forces. The moral code existing in a given era was, in his view, an expression of the prevailing mode of production, an attempt by the "haves" to protect their vested interests and maintain the status quo. Based as all such codes were on exploitation—of woman by man, slave by master, serf by nobleman, worker by capitalist—they had no binding force at all.

Marx felt that at the time of his writing, the mid-nineteenth century, the stage was set for the Revolution. Capitalistic exploitation had created a proletariat ready to throw off its chains and establish the Classless Society. In this final synthesis of the dialectic, the proletarian ethic would take over. There would be an end of private ownership; people would lose their acquisitive tendencies and look upon the goods of the earth as being for all. There would be a pervasive sense of community; men would be aware of their fellowship with one another as no exploited worker, forced to grub for a livelihood, could ever be. The goal of the new society would be, not just the production of goods, as in the asocial, bourgeois states of the nineteenth century, but of good men.

The Proletarian Revolution was inevitable, according to Marx, but its outbreak could be hastened. The proletariat could be stirred up and made so resentful of their lot that they would tolerate it no longer. Fostering discontent among the underprivileged, the disenfranchised, the oppressed is in fact the assigned

46

task of Communist party members throughout the world. Any act, be it murder, sedition, lying, theft, bribery, treachery, calculated to aid communism is right and good in their view. "From the point of view of Communist morality," Lenin wrote, " 'moral' is only that which strengthens the new Communist regime."[17]

For William James, the morality prevalent in any given period was the product of social pressure.[18] While it continues to suit the people's needs, it remains in force, but there is nothing necessary or immutable about it. Just as it came into being through popular insistence, so through the same agency can it be changed or discarded. The ethician, like the physical scientist, must therefore keep an eye on the passing scene and be ready to revise his positions from day to day. Long-accepted values enjoy a certain a priori favor, of course, and every change involves a certain amount of risk, so the philosopher should try to preserve as much of the "traditionally recognized good" as possible. But he should not consider any moral principle absolute or inviolable. When the pressure gets too great he should yield, his norm for estimating the value of a new law or custom always being "how much more outcry or how much appeasement comes about" by reason of it.

For James, morality was essentially social. A solitary thinker could adopt whatever principles of conduct he pleased, and they would be neither right nor wrong; he had only to be consistent in applying them. But when another person invades his moral solitude the moral question arises, because this other can make a claim upon him and, for James, "Claim and obligation are co-extensive terms; they cover each other exactly. . . . Without a claim actually made by some concrete person there can be no obligation . . . there is some obligation wherever there is such a claim." The validity of the claim was not to be questioned; it was intrinsic to the claim itself. Any claim ought "for its own sole sake, to be satisfied."

John Dewey also conceived morality as being purely social.[19] Conscience for him was essentially a knowing *with*, and one had always to consider the effect on others before reaching a decision on what was right or wrong. Indeed, in his view, the moral question arose only because our actions affect others who have the physical power to make us suffer for any injury we do them. For Dewey, the question "Why be moral?" ultimately had the same answer as the question "Why take my hand off a hot stove?": "You'll get hurt if you don't." Right in his view was "the totality of social pressure."

CRITIQUE

Nietzsche's enfranchisement of the strong to engage in whatever bloodletting is necessary for them to secure their natural ascendancy over the weak is less a moral theory than a denial of morality. If the weak have no rights, would not the less strong lack them too, so that the massacre would continue until the pecking order was established down to its ultimate refinement?

To justify the onslaught, Nietzsche appeals to nature's purpose in endowing the strong with precisely the attributes necessary for success. But, though this teleological approach to morality has its place—as when Aristotle argued that, since nature had endowed man with the faculty of speech, she must have meant that he live in the company of his fellows—Nietzsche's use of it is questionable. It can hardly be said that, because some people are naturally stronger, more ruthless, and more cunning than others, nature therefore sanctions their use of these endowments to make themselves masters of the world. Men are essentially equal, after all; nature makes no man another's slave. Then too, a man's moral character is more manifest in the

48

kindliness he shows the unfortunate than in the advantage he takes of their plight.

Nietzsche's categorizing of the Jews as a weak race is by no means evident, either. Jacob's sons surely showed no lack of guile and ruthlessness in revenging the rape of their sister Dinah by Shechem, son of Hamor the Hivite. Moses, the great Jewish leader, once became so enraged at seeing an Egyptian strike a Hebrew that he killed the fellow—hardly a sign of weakness by Nietzsche's standards! Having received the Ten Commandments, the Jewish people went on to fight their way quite valorously to the Promised Land. The many breakthroughs Jews have made, particularly in psychiatry, mathematics, physics, and medicine, make untenable the charge that they are an intellectually inferior race. It has in fact been suggested that the mistreatment of them by the Nazis was prompted more by envy than contempt.

Nor does history bear out Nietzsche's thesis that Christianity is a religion of the weak. One remembers in this connection Clovis' remark when St. Rémi finished reading to him the gospel account of Christ's passion and death: "Ah! If only I had been there with my Franks!" Such Christianity, militant even to the point of preventing the redemption of mankind, is, we rather feel, more characteristic of Christ's followers than the tendency to turn the other cheek. Not that we have any doubt, Nietzsche notwithstanding, that this takes considerably more moral strength than lashing back.

Spencer's moral theory, tempered as it is by his high regard for altruism and his willingness to let nature take its course rather than sanction any blitzkrieg upon the unfit, is somewhat less brutal than Nietzsche's. Only somewhat, however, as is apparent from the vogue it enjoyed with the rugged individualists and robber barons of the late nineteenth century who were putting into practice precisely what he advocated in theory. Several of these individuals invited Spencer to America in 1882. John D. Rockefeller, one of his hosts, once remarked in a Sunday school address:

> The growth of a large business is merely a survival of the fittest.
> . . . The American Beauty rose can be produced in the splendor and fragrance which bring cheer to its beholder only by sacrificing the early buds which grow up around it. This is not an evil tendency in business. It is merely the working-out of a law of nature and a law of God.[20]

Our thought is that, though pruning and weeding have their place where roses are concerned, they do not apply to human beings. It is difficult to understand how the altruistic, who alone, according to Spencer, are slated for survival, can stand aside and make no effort to help the unfortunate or insist that the civil authorities do so. Yet this is exactly what they are supposed to do; since nature has declared war on the unfit, to impede her efforts at purifying the race would be to interfere with the basic law of nature, the survival of the fittest.

For Spencer, government exists only to protect the citizen's life, freedom, and property, to enforce contracts, and to keep public order. It has no business meddling in the marketplace, the only control there being the law of supply and demand. He opposed any social or economic legislation that would place the state on the side of the unfit. He was against poor laws, state-supported education, sanitary supervision, even a government postal system!

Spencer's advocacy of political laissez-faire followed logically from his thesis that men are on trial. "If they are sufficiently complete to live, they *do* live, and it is well they should live. If they are not sufficiently complete to live, they die, and it is best they should die." He was highly optimistic that nature's campaign against the unfit would one day succeed:

> The ultimate development of the ideal man is logically certain—
> as certain as any conclusion in which we place the most implicit
> faith; for instance that all men will die. . . . Progress, therefore,
> is not an accident, but a necessity. Instead of civilization being
> artificial, it is a part of nature; all of a piece with the develop-
> ment of the embryo or the unfolding of a flower.[21]

Spencer's confidence on this point stemmed from his acceptance of the Lamarckian thesis that acquired mental and physical characteristics can be transmitted from parent to child.
Lamarckianism has been long since discredited, however, and
indeed it is quite evident that the blacksmith cannot pass on his
bulging muscles to his son, nor the man of learning his knowledge. There is, in fact, a good deal of truth in the old French
adage about *le fils inconnu d'un père célèbre.* Whatever became,
one wonders, of Lord Chesterfield's son, to whom so brilliant a
father addressed so much salutary advice?

Spencer, and evolutionary moral theorists generally, make
the moral value of an act depend upon the existing stage of evolution; it becomes good because it here and now helps men ad-
just to their environment. It is difficult to see, however, how
evolutionary forces, materialistic, impersonal, and amoral as
they presumably are, can be determinative of moral value.
There appears to be here a violation of the principle that
"A thing cannot give what it does not have" or "The effect cannot exceed the cause."

Though Marx accepted evolutionary theory in general,
the thought of nature declaring war on a certain class of people
offended his humanitarian sensibilities. In his view, nature was
man's ally, not his enemy. Man was, in fact, part of nature and
could achieve his full humanity only through involvement with
matter. What Marx wanted was for him to be properly related
to nature: as a person, not a thing.

Now, just how the notion of person—at least in the Scholastic sense of an individual substance of a rational (and therefore spiritual) nature—fits into a materialism of the Marxist genre is difficult to see. If man is continuous with nature, on what basis does his special dignity rest? The same problem arises with Marx's doctrine on free will. He says that man is free, yet is part of nature which is determined; the Revolution is inevitable, yet Marxists leave no stone unturned to hasten its advent. There appears here a conflict between free will and determinism.

Marx held the moral code existing in his time had no validity, yet he condemned the exploitation of the working class in terms of it. When he said it was unjust, wrong, and so forth, for capitalists to abuse laborers, he expected people to agree with him. Many did, of course, for he was right; it is in fact ironic that the most effective condemnation of nineteenth-century economic injustice came, not from any churchman, but from a materialist who believed in no life but the present. Our point is only that, in decrying the social and economic inequities that existed in his time, he took his stand upon the very moral code he rejected.

The Revolution Marx considered imminent did not occur on the worldwide scale he predicted. A workers' revolution occurred in Russia, and the Communist party took over its leadership, but the utopia Marx had in mind has not materialized. Ivan shows little willingness to give his all for the community or to subordinate his interests entirely to the common good. If he could be induced to work as hard on the collective farm as he does on his own little plot, the produce of which he can keep for himself, the food-shortage problem would soon be solved. When the commissars want things done efficiently and with dispatch, such as getting missiles off the ground and into orbit, they attract the best talent available by the old capitalist device of offering higher wages. It hardly seems, then, that the motive of private gain has lost its power under communism. Indeed, the present vogue of Evsei Liberman's economic policies, featuring as they do decentralized planning and profit motivation, indicates that the USSR is rediscovering capitalism.

Even bourgeois morality is back in favor. In the days immediately following the Revolution, easy marriage and even easier divorce was the policy, on the Marxist principle that marriage was a bourgeois institution whose chief purpose was to ensure the orderly transfer of property from father to son. From 1917 to 1922, couples had only to appear before the local registrar and declare themselves married; if things did not work out, they had only to see him again and declare themselves divorced. "What that led to we all know," dourly remarked two Soviet lawyers in the course of a frank discussion of the marital chaos the experiment in pure Marxism occasioned in Russia.[22] A new law, enacted in February 1968, requires that marriage be formally contracted and makes divorce proceedings both lengthy and expensive.

The difficulties encountered by the Soviet authorities in putting Marxism into practice spring from its weakness as a theory—its erroneous concept of the nature of man and of morality. Though man is continuous with the material world as regards his body, the human soul is a spiritual principle. And, important as economic forces are, they do not determine what is right and wrong, but are themselves subject to such determination. The working-class exploitation which Marx condemned was as wrong in the mid-nineteenth century as it is clearly seen to be now. It did not become wrong when it was no longer economically necessary; it was wrong—immoral, that is, of itself and intrinsically—by reason of its denial of human dignity. Marxism fails to give an adequate account of this dignity and of the higher law that reigns supreme even over economic forces.

The teaching of James and Dewey that morality governs man only in his relations with others is not at all evident, either. A man has certain duties to himself which would obtain even if he were the only one alive, the positive obligation of preserving his life, for example, and the negative one of not committing suicide. In particular, James' thesis that the moral law has its origin in the claims made upon us by others lacks cogency. Not only can moral obligation exist without any claim at all, but as Sesonske has pointed out, only such claims as are valid need be honored.[23]

It is difficult to see, too, how both James and Dewey failed to recognize the existence of moral absolutes. Even if one draws one's moral theory from quotidian facts, as Dewey would have us do, it takes very little genius or experience to realize that life and reputation, for example, are values which force themselves upon us, so that we necessarily prize them and consider any attack upon them, in the form of murder or libel, inherently wrong. No amount of social pressure can change that, for the esteem man has of these values is deeply imbedded in his nature.

Our conviction is, however, that though James and Dewey explicitly deny moral absolutes, they implicitly affirm them. For James, a claim was an absolute, to be honored without question, and for him whatever promoted the happiness of the community was by that fact good—inherently and absolutely. Dewey's awareness of absolutes is evident from his constant use of words like *growth, development,* and *progress,* which have meaning only in terms of an objective standard. And, though he makes social pressure the source of right, this was never for him a random or uncontrolled force. It became the "road to good," he said, when "the elements that compose this unremitting pressure are enlightened, . . . as social relationships become themselves reasonable." Men of genius and talent were supposed to be constantly trying to solve community problems so that social pressure never became seriously disruptive of the established order.

54

Dewey's explicit rejection of absolutes had its basis in his abhorrence of a moral apriorism and voluntarism which attempts to make morality merely a matter of loyalty to a Supreme Being and a defense of otherworldly values totally unrelated to the human situation. The maxim *fiat justitia, ruat coelum* made no sense to him; any act that brought about natural disasters was no virtue in his eyes. For him, an act was morally good when it improved—he preferred to say ameliorated—the lot of mankind.

Dewey made value begin with enjoyment because he considered this the only way to avoid what he called the "pallid remoteness of the rationalistic theory" with its insistence on "transcendental values." Of itself, however, enjoyment merely made the thing a "problematic value"; reason had then to enter in and determine whether it was truly valuable. Dewey located his moral theory in-between what he called the "transcendent theory of *a priori* ideas" and a utilitarianism which makes mere enjoyment the standard of moral value. This, we are inclined to think, is where a moral theory belongs. It is exactly where Socrates placed it with his theory that whatever promotes man's true happiness is good. Aristotle, too, though he found an indication of immortality in the active intellect, confined his speculations on the happy life to the present one here on earth.

Thus, though we reject the various pressure theories because of their moral relativism and general inability to account for the facts of moral consciousness, we find great merit in the contention of James and Dewey that the moral law arises out of the human situation, out of what man finds good and valuable. In particular we appreciate Dewey's thesis that reason, "always an honorific term in ethics," is man's guide to what is truly valuable. Indeed, the thought occurs that, in the end, reason was Dewey's norm of morality.

55

AUTONOMOUS REASON

AS THE NORM

Kant, deeply impressed with the "moral law within," paid little heed to the suggestion that pleasure was its norm. If man were meant only to enjoy himself, then nature would have made instinct the dominant human faculty, since it is far more efficient in the pursuit of pleasure than reason. Kant held, in fact, that the more a man lives the life of reason, the more he resents reason because of the sacrifices it requires of him and tends toward "misology," the hatred of reason. A reasonable being had only to look within himself, however, to realize that reason is his guide to goodness and that the moral law is in essence the law of reason.

KANT'S MORAL THEORY

Kant found this law characterized by universality and necessity; lying as such was wrong and could not under any circumstances be permissible for a rational being. Now, universality and necessity were for him "sure signs of *a priori* knowledge";[1] knowledge of this kind could not be derived from experience. Experience tells us only what is, not what has to be. The cow of experience is, perhaps, white, but cows can be black or brown, too, and furthermore it is always this cow, never cow as such. Experience, in other words, deals only with the contingent and the singular.

The moral law, then, being both universal and necessary, had to originate within the rational being himself; knowledge of it had to be completely a priori, independent of experience. This meant to Kant that practical reason, which is to say, reason dealing with matters of moral choice and decision—Scholastics would call it the will, and Kant sometimes makes this identification, too—was autonomous, a law unto itself. In issuing its categorical imperatives, reason consulted nothing outside itself; no empirical element entered into its deliberations, not the fact that I am married and a father, or even that I am a man. Only so, Kant felt, could the moral law be kept pure and valid for all rational beings, some of whom might conceivably not be human.

Inevitably, morality became for Kant a matter of logical consistency. It was wrong to lie because the liar acts illogically. He takes advantage of the general practice of truth-telling but does not abide by it himself; he lies but does not wish to be lied to. The same with stealing; the last thing the thief wants is to be stolen from. Suicide was wrong because anyone who kills himself uses the very instinct meant to preserve life in order to end it and therefore acts as if life were the same as nonlife.

The liar, the thief, and the suicide fail to show proper regard for the universality of the moral law. They act as if it applied to others but not to them. Since it is in fact universal in its application, one should always be able to base one's action on a maxim which would be acceptable as a general moral principle. The most fundamental of these is: "I am never to act otherwise than so that I can also will that my maxim should become a universal law."[2] Kant called this ultimate categorical imperative the "Universal Law of Nature."

Kant saw man, and indeed every rational being, as an end in himself. This led him to the formulation of his second practical principle: "Act so that in your person as well as in the person of every other you are treating mankind also as an end, never merely as a means."[3] One might in good conscience hire another person as a servant, since this does not negate his dignity as a rational being, but one must not enslave him. The principle ruled out murder and suicide, too, for when one kills a person, whether oneself or another, one makes him a mere means to some nonabsolute end. Kant even considered it wrong for a state to maintain a standing army, since this subordinated men to the achievement of arbitrary national goals.

Kant held that a rational being's proper vocation was to fulfill his moral duty completely and thus achieve a good will. But, though practical reason commands this, the tension between man's empirical and rational self militates against its attainment. In practice, people tend to act out of desire and self-love rather than in accord with the dictates of reason. A "good will" was therefore "a perfection of which no rational being of the sensible world is capable at any moment of its existence."[4]

This did not mean that death ended the matter. Since achieving a good will was the proper goal of a rational being, the pursuit of it had to go on forever. Kant held the moral law therefore postulates—which is to say, demands or logically necessitates—immortality. Though pure reason can discover no necessary connection between rationality and immortality, practical reason requires it, because without immortality the rational being's call to morality would lack a sound practical basis.

CAMROSE LUTHERAN COLLEGE LIBRARY

BJ
1012
.M 317 | 21,068

Morality also postulated freedom. The two notions, freedom and morality, were, in fact, "so inseparably united," Kant held, "that one might define practical freedom as independence of the will on anything but the moral law alone."[5] Freedom was the indispensable condition of the categorical imperative, and was therefore the second postulate of practical reason.

Lastly, morality postulated God. Not as Lawgiver, for according to Kant a will, to be free, had to be self-legislating; autonomy was a corollary of freedom. To introduce heteronomy into morality was to destroy its very nature. It gave rise to the question "Why should I obey?" or "How does obedience profit me?" and such questions had no place where morality was concerned. The moral law was absolute, to be obeyed for no other reason than that it was the law; one was to do one's duty simply because it was one's duty. Kant wrote: "Morality, in so far as it is grounded in the concept of man as a being who is free but at the same time subjects himself through his reason to unconditional laws, needs neither the idea of another being above man for the latter to recognize his duty, nor any other motive than the law itself for man to fulfill his duty."[6]

Kant felt that morality postulated God as a moral ideal, one in whom there existed no disinclination toward the fulfillment of duty, no need of self-conquest. The will of God was not just good, but holy; it was the standard on which rational beings should model themselves. Thus, though no proof of God's existence could satisfy the rigorous demands of pure reason, practical reason postulated it.

CRITIQUE

A *Kant's Absolutism*

One does not lightly undertake a critique of Kantianism. Schlick criticized Kant for insisting on the absolute character of moral obligation.[7] For him, there could no more be an "absolute ought" than an "absolute uncle." Just as uncle implies a nephew

59

or a niece, so ought implies a demand made upon one person by another who is able to "reward fulfillment and to punish neglect." Kant, we feel, had a far more valid notion of the nature of moral obligation. Moral imperatives are indeed categorical, not hypothetical, and the moral aspect of the human act has nothing to do with reward or punishment. It is not Kant who distorts the notion of ought, in our opinion, but Schlick.

Schlick also attacked Kant, and absolutists in general, for having no ultimate answer to the question "What do these objective values mean to *me*?" or "Why should I accept them as *my* moral guidelines?" He thought any proper answer must take into account the problem of "What happens to me if I don't?" For him, morality had ultimately to rely upon subjective feelings, upon desire or what is good for me. Thus, anyone who could spend a happy life as a scoundrel—if that were possible, considering that society tends to deal quite harshly with such people—would have no reason at all to be moral. Kant's position on this point appears unassailable, however. Man is indeed intuitively aware that he is called to morality, that the acquisition of a good will is the human vocation, so that the question of "What happens to me if I don't?" is beside the point.

B *Kant's Postulates*

Kant has also been criticized for being inexcusably pragmatic in postulating God, free will, and immortality. In his *Critique of Pure Reason* he declared all three of these propositions undemonstrable, going even so far as to hold that, since they constitute the principal themes of metaphysics, this was an "impossible science." And yet, in his *Critique of Practical Reason*, when he found that, without them, morality lacked a sound practical basis, they suddenly become "postulates."

This makes Kant's postulates sound like mere ad hoc inventions, concocted to suit the need of the moment. They are more than that, however; as we have seen, Kant felt the moral law

60

demands or logically necessitates them. When he postulates God's existence, for example, he says:

> The laws of morality do not merely presuppose the existence of a supreme being, but postulate it with right (though only, of course, from the practical point of view), as these laws are themselves absolutely necessary in another relation.[8]

One might wish that Kant had proceeded from the "moral law within" which, he said, was "not a postulate, but a law," to the reality of what it logically implied or necessitated: the existence of God, the fact of both free will and immortality. And, in fact, he seems to have considered this quite seriously. In his *Critique of Practical Reason* he wrote:

> Through the idea of the supreme good as object and final end of the pure practical reason the moral law leads to religion, that is, to the recognition of all duties as divine commands, *not as sanctions, that is, as arbitrary commands of an alien will which are contingent in themselves,* but as essential *laws* of every free will in itself, which, however, must be looked on as commands of the Supreme Being, because it is only from a morally perfect (holy and good) and at the same time all-powerful will, and consequently only through harmony with this will, that we can hope to attain the highest good, which the moral law makes it our duty to take as the object of our endeavour.[9]

It appears from the *Opus Postumum* that, toward the end of his life, Kant was particularly intrigued with the Deontological Argument, which gets to God's existence from the moral absolutes found in conscience. Among his jottings this observation appears: "In the moral practical reason lies the categorical imperative to regard all human duties as divine commands."[10] And this: "the concept of God is the concept of an obligation-imposing subject outside myself."[11] And, lastly, this: "Freedom under laws; duties as divine commands. There is a God."[12] While it is of course impossible to say how Kant would have integrated these notations into his system, they cannot be dismissed merely as the random thoughts of an old man. It has in fact been suggested that he meant to substitute a new type of metaphysics for the one he had demolished in his *Critique of Pure Reason*, one based on the demands of practical reason.[13]

Kant of course always had the inhibiting influence of Hume to contend with. Hume had, he said, awakened him from his "dogmatic slumbers," putting him on his guard against metaphysical demonstrations which went beyond experience and reached conclusions which, though logical, might not be true. Fear of mentalism, making the laws of thought the laws of being, kept him from attributing to reality what he saw logically implied by the "moral law within." It is of interest to note the much fuller use Newman, who had no such inhibitions, made of the data of moral consciousness.

For Newman, moral absolutes clearly revealed the existence of an Absolute Being.[14] They related his soul, he said, to a "tribunal over which it has no power." This Absolute Being whose existence conscience made "luminously self-evident" to him had to be a personal being because otherwise there was no accounting for the feeling of shame consequent upon doing wrong. One does not, after all, "feel shame before a horse or a dog."

c *Kant's Formalism*

Kant felt he had to keep his moral theory pure: uncontaminated, that is, by any empirical element. If the moral law was to be valid, not just for men, but for all rational beings, no contingent consideration of time or circumstance, not even the fact that this rational being happens to be human, could have anything to do with it. This law had to be simply the product of reason, purely a priori.

This is high idealism, to be sure, but it puts morality beyond the reach of men who must live in a world of space and time. It gives them no way of determining the material content of their duty or what it is here and now. Kant says they must never make themselves exceptions to the moral law and always be able to base their actions on maxims which would be acceptable as guiding principles for all. But he gives them no norm for judging whether they should or should not will that a given maxim become a universal law. How can they know, for example, on a purely a priori basis, whether lying or stealing would be acceptable as a general practice? It takes a certain amount of experience to realize that these activities make social life difficult if not impossible.

Hegel noted that, despite Kant's efforts to keep his moral theory pure, certain empirical elements crept into it. For example, in demonstrating the obligation of returning entrusted property, Kant said that to refuse to do so would mean involving oneself in the contradiction that property is nonproperty. But, Hegel remarks, this follows only if it is possible to establish a priori that there is some necessary connection between man's rational nature and the ownership of property. This, he held, cannot be done. Indeed, one might, he suggested, just as well adopt the premise that there is no such thing as property, that nonproperty is nonproperty and be an entirely consistent—and therefore, on Kantian terms, a perfectly moral—thief![15] Hegel's point was that the moral law cannot be evolved on a purely a priori basis, that experience was needed for its determination.

This, in fact, seems quite obvious. An action's unacceptability as a general practice is not the factor precisely determinative of its malice. One would not appreciate it if everyone were to go driving on the highway at the same precise moment, thus creating a monumental traffic jam, but this would not make doing so immoral. One feels that Kant's condemnation of murder and theft as immoral needs—and, as Hegel notes, actually had —a more empirical foundation than the mere lack of logic involved in making oneself an exception to the law. How, one wonders, if he were faithful to his own norm, did Kant feel free to become a philosopher? Should he not have been deterred by the thought that, if everybody did, there would be no one to bake the bread? His no-exception rule, it seems evident, is not susceptible of universal application.

D *Duty and Moral Value*

Then too, Kant's thesis that only acts done out of respect for law have moral value denies such value to acts which go beyond the call of duty. The common opinion is, however, that acts of heroism, generosity, and self-sacrifice are morally nobler than those which are strictly obligatory. It is in fact anomalous that Kant, who esteemed freedom so highly as to identify it with autonomy, saw moral value only in the surrender of it to grim duty, and left no room in his moral theory for true love and ardent generosity.

Because of these deficiences in Kant's moral theory, but with profound respect for his insistence that the moral law is essentially the law of reason, we must look further for the norm of morality.

RIGHT REASON AS THE NORM

 Kant's teaching that, for a rational being, the moral law is the law of reason seems evident enough. Though we do not often advert to it, we are all aware that our basic obligation is to listen to reason. We disapprove of the sadist's penchant for inflicting pain on others because we feel people should seek pleasure in a reasonable way. We do not feel obliged to follow every health fad that comes along, but only to take a reasonable care of our health. When a jury is convinced beyond a reasonable doubt that the defendant committed the crime, they feel justified in finding him guilty.

Reason is so clearly the rational being's guide to goodness that no other norm can be proposed without affirming it. When Epicurus identified the good with the pleasurable, he at once set out to prove that this was the only sensible outlook on life. Hobbes did not just assert that the sovereign will was the norm of morality; he had a reason—it was the only way to avoid anarchy. And so of all the others. Whatever norm is explicitly proposed, there is always a more ultimate appeal to reason. We, too, throughout the entire discussion on the norm of morality, have been assuming that reason is the norm. We have rejected the various proposed norms because they contained inner contradictions or did not square with the facts of moral consciousness; in other words, because they did not satisfy the demands of reason.

The Ayer-Toulmin debate on the role reason plays in reaching ethical conclusions deserves mention here.[1] Toulmin concedes that the statement "Stealing is wrong" has certain imperative overtones such as "Don't steal!" or "Stealing? Naughty!" He grants, too, that, viewed as commands, ethical statements are neither true nor false but calls to action. When the sergeant major bawls, "Stand to attention!" one does not, he says, wonder whether he is telling the truth or not; one acts.

He insists, however, that even commands have a basis in reason. A child, told to take off his muddy shoes before going into the drawing room, may ask, "Why?" and will be told that his mother does not want him to dirty the carpet. This, Toulmin says, is a reason, and a good one, while the reply, "Because it's the third Tuesday before Pentecost" would be a poor one. The same is true, he holds, of moral statements, viewed merely as commands: even if "Stealing is wrong" means nothing more than "Don't steal," the one who says it has his reasons.

For Toulmin, however, ethical statements are more than just commands. The initial error of Ayer's "imperative doctrine," he says, is that it "treats ethical statements, which approximate in some respects to commands and interjections, as if they were just commands and interjections." It compounds this error when it goes on to "dismiss all evaluative inferences as beyond the scope of reasoning." We do in fact give reasons for evaluative statements, he insists. When we say, for example, that a man who beats his wife is wicked, we are not just saying that he beats his wife or telling him to stop it; we are saying it is wrong for him to do so and condemning him for it. Asked to defend our position, we point out that he is not his wife's master, nor she his slave, that he would not like to be beaten himself, and so forth. Our evaluative judgment, therefore, is not arbitrary or merely emotional; it has a rational basis.

Toulmin sees no point in allowing the discussion to get bogged down in mere semantics. If the defenders of the imperative doctrine would prefer that some term other than *reasoning* be applied to the process by which one proceeds from factual premises to ethical conclusions, he is willing to humor them. He is rather sure, however, that, if they are just ignored, they will soon find something else to occupy them. The Greeks, he says, paid no attention to Anaxagoras' contention that they should not speak of things as "coming into being" and "passing away," but rather as being "mixed" and "separated." No particular harm befell them, and the philosophers turned their attention elsewhere. Just so, Toulmin suggests, if we refuse to consider ethical judgments as mere ejaculations and continue to give reasons for them, all the imperativists can do is evince disapproval, whether they feel it or not!

Our thesis that reason is the norm of morality is admittedly neither new nor startling; we have merely made explicit what anyone with the use of reason knows at least implicitly. Indeed, had we unearthed anything obscure and unheard-of in such a familiar field as morality, it would be at once suspect. Since the pursuit of moral goodness is the human vocation, it would be strange if ordinary people did not have at least a general idea of what constitutes it. The ancient Greeks, as we have mentioned, saw clearly the relationship between knowledge and virtue. For them, the good was also the true; the virtuous man was one who knew the true good and was guided by that knowledge. Aristotle wrote:

> Virtue then is a settled disposition of the mind determining the choice of actions and emotions, consisting essentially in the observance of the mean relative to us, this being determined by principle (*logos*), that is, as the prudent man would determine it.[2]

St. Thomas put it this way:

> In human actions, good and evil are predicated in relation to the reason because, as Dionysius says, the good of man is to be in accord with reason, and evil is to be against reason. For that is good for a thing which suits it according to its form; and evil, that which is against the order of its form. It is therefore evident that the difference of good and evil, considered in reference to the object, is an essential difference in relation to reason, i.e., according as the object is suitable or unsuitable to reason. Now, certain actions are called human or moral inasmuch as they proceed from the reason.[3]

THE OBJECTIVE NORM

Kant made reason a law unto itself. For St. Thomas, however, it mediated between the person and reality—not reason alone, but right reason was the norm of morality. Reason, to be right, had to conform its judgment to certain objective truths: the fact that man is a being composed of body and soul, dependent upon God, equal to his neighbor and, as a person, superior to material things. Suarez summed up these truths, which are normative for man, in the phrase "human nature adequately considered."[4]

For these two Scholastic thinkers, Aquinas and Suarez, the entire moral law arose out of these truths. Murder was wrong because one who kills another unjustly plays God. He acts as if

68

he were that person's lord and master, when in fact he is not. Theft was wrong because one who steals another's property acts as if the other were his slave, obligated to labor for him and supply him with goods when in fact all men are equal. To us, this derivation of the moral law from the complete truth about man makes good sense; since action follows being, what one ought to do should be determined by what one is.

IDEALISM AND MORALITY

We have said that reason is man's guide to moral good-ness, the standard of moral value. Some would hold, however, that it is only a minimal standard: a help in learning what one's absolute obligations are, but irrelevant in the upper reaches of morality where it is more a matter of idealism and heroism than of merely fulfilling the law. The man who refuses to enter a burning building in order to save a child may act reasonably, they say, but he would do better to throw caution to the winds and risk his life.

Bergson's Theory

Bergson held this view. He opposed what he called the Kantian cult of reason. Reason, he conceded, recognizes and ratifies the basic rules of social living, but these do not constitute morality properly so-called. They are merely a "system of orders dictated by impersonal social requirements" which is "in its original and fundamental elements subrational."[1] Instinct, he pointed out, leads a colony of ants to adopt essentially the same procedures.

For Bergson, the morality proper to man was suprarational and incapable of being reduced to "dead, impersonal formulae"; it was a call to be heroic, and heroism cannot be legislated or preached. It must show itself in action, become incarnate to a significant degree in some leader who then serves as a model for the rest of mankind. Men cast in this heroic mold have not been lacking in the course of world history. Bergson wrote:

> Before the saints of Christianity, mankind has known the sages of Greece, the prophets of Israel, the Arahants of Buddhism, and others besides. It is to them that men have always turned for that complete morality which we had best call absolute morality.

Above them all, he said, there towers the heroic figure of Christ:

> If the great mystics are indeed such as we have described them, they are the imitators, original but incomplete continuators, of what Christ of the Gospels was completely.[2]

Bergson's hero made the difference between what Newman termed a mere notional assent, which offers no stimulus to action because its object is an abstraction, and a real assent, which is given to something concrete, here to a person. The hero concretizes concepts like "loyalty, sacrifice of self, the spirit of renunciation, charity," which until his coming were merely words, only vaguely understood, lying undigested on the mind. "But only let these formulae be invested with substance, and that substance become animate, lo and behold! a new life is proclaimed; we understand, we feel the advent of a new morality."[3] The hero stirs an "emotion which drives the intelligence forward in spite of obstacles."[4] The call-of-the-hero is not just for the chosen few, either; it is for all. "There is a mystic dormant within us, merely waiting for an occasion to awake."[5]

Von Hildebrand's Theory

Von Hildebrand also opposes the thesis that reason is the norm of morality. He in fact thinks the conformity-to-nature approach can easily lead to misconceptions as to what is right and wrong. Avarice, debauchery, and promiscuity suit our natural tendencies rather well, he points out, but they are immoral. His own view is that man does not learn what is good by first considering his nature; on the contrary, he knows what he is by experiencing his call to the good. Von Hildebrand writes:

> In order to grasp that an act of justice is good, or injustice evil, or that fidelity is morally noble, infidelity morally base, we do not need to analyze the nature of man. On the contrary . . . in order to grasp the truth that man is destined to be morally good and that this is not merely a factual trend but also an objective relation of "oughtness," we must first of all know moral values . . . the insight into the goodness of justice reveals to us that man is destined to partake of this goodness.[6]

Von Hildebrand's approach to morality is teleological; virtue attracts the person and evokes an affective response. Not that he reduces moral attitudes to the level of sensation, as did the Earl of Shaftsbury with his "Moral Sense" Theory. Von Hildebrand carefully distinguishes between spiritual affectivity and mere emotion, between our joy when a man forgives his enemy and our sense of euphoria when the weather is fine and the digestion good. The word *feeling* applied to these diverse experiences is, he says, analogous if not actually equivocal, the one being spiritual, the other physical and animalistic. To regard all

72

feeling or affectivity as merely emotional is a gross error, he contends; it is like saying that because some knowledge is in the sense order there is no such thing as intellectual or spiritual knowledge.

Von Hildebrand is not satisfied merely at having affectivity placed on a par with reason and will in the discovery of moral value; he would have it accorded the primacy. Our admiration of a morally excellent act—of mercy, say, or generosity—does not, he claims, proceed from mind or will but from the heart. We do not first consider our nature to see whether it is proper or reasonable to admire such an act, nor do we choose or decide to do so. Our reaction is spontaneous, demanded—necessitated, even—by the appeal of the moral value involved. Von Hildebrand calls it a "heart response."

Since the heart response is "not in itself free,"[7] the question arises: How can acts prompted by it have moral value? Von Hildebrand's answer is that one can "say yes" to the heart's instinctive love of the good and make it one's own, or "say no" and nullify it. Since the response comes under the indirect control of the will in this way, he says, acts done in virtue of it have moral value.

CRITIQUE

Bergson and Von Hildebrand have done well to emphasize the positive and teleological side of morality. Virtue is indeed more a matter of inspiration than of obligation, immorality more a failure to love than a refusal to obey. To the well-disposed, virtue speaks loudly and clearly, and its appeal is all but irresistible. Children are particularly sensitive to it, a fact of which *McGuffey's Readers* took full advantage. Young Americans did not have to be told that little George Washington did the right thing when he admitted to his father he had chopped down the cherry tree; they easily discerned the presence of moral value in the act and felt their own call to virtue.

Von Hildebrand has rightly insisted on the spiritual aspect of affectivity and its importance in moral theory. Charity surely has more moral value when it proceeds warmly from the heart rather than coldly from the head. The Good Samaritan was the better man for having been moved with compassion over the plight of the man bleeding in the roadside ditch than if he had administered a charity dictated by reason alone. Despite Kant, one feels there is more moral value in a good act done out of natural inclination than one done solely as a matter of grim duty.

One can concede all this, however, and still not agree with Bergson's or Von Hildebrand's removal of morality from the jurisdiction of reason. Reason can operate unobtrusively in the background but still be in charge. There are indeed people of such obviously heroic mold, so undeniably noble and self-sacrificing, that there is no question but that we should follow them. And there are acts which are so clearly virtuous that we cannot fail to recognize them as such and rejoice at their performance.

When doubt arises, however, as to the moral value of the virtue one has been practicing or the heroism of the person one has been following, reason at once asserts its authority and decides the issue on the basis of fact and principle, not aesthetic appeal. This is rather clear evidence that it has been monitoring the situation all the time, gratefully accepting the help of affectivity when it was available, but not relying on it as the norm of right action.

Marriage provides a case in point. For married people who are in love, there is no temptation toward adultery, no thought of divorce. It may even be true, as Von Hildebrand says, that one can learn from such a marriage what the marital relationship really means. The fact remains, however, that marital morality is the same whether this affection exists or not; it is the product of reason reflecting on the human situation.

CAMROSE LUTHERAN COLLEGE LIBRARY

Bergson protests his "admiration for the speculative function of the mind," but thinks that "when philosophers maintain that it would be sufficient to silence selfishness and passion, they prove to us . . . that they have never heard the voice of the one or the other very loud within themselves."[8] This may well be, but then, would the person who is selfish or passionately aroused be any more likely to heed the call-of-the-hero than to listen to reason? In any case, what we are in search of is a norm of morality, not a remedy for concupiscence. We are concerned, not with how to induce people to be good, but with what makes a human act good. This, we continue to hold, is its reasonableness: no human act can have moral value if it is contrary to reason. One may risk one's life to save another, but the situation must warrant it; there must always be a reasonable chance of succeeding. There is no virtue, objectively speaking, in recklessly throwing one's life away.

VIII

THE NATURAL LAW

The natural law is so-called because it arises out of human nature. There are other natures, of course—the bovine, equine, feline, and so forth—and each imposes upon the individual possessing it a certain *modus agendi*, a law for that nature. As Ulpian said:

> [T]his law is not proper to the human race, but to all animals found on earth and in the sea and to the birds, too.[1]

The kind of obligation which the natural law imposes upon free subjects differs, however, from the kind it imposes upon those that are physically necessitated. Since the concept of law is fully verified only when the subject remains free to follow its mandates or not, we shall in future restrict the term *natural law* to that which flows from human nature.

MORAL ABSOLUTES

Reason, reflecting on the human situation, recognizes that there are certain moral absolutes: truths to be respected under all circumstances, values to be safeguarded come what may. It sees that to violate these truths or deny these values to oneself or another is intrinsically evil, that murder, theft, libel, and the like, are wrong by reason of their object: because what is done violates the truth of what man is or constitutes an attack on a basic human value.

SITUATION ETHICS

Some moralists deny there are any moral absolutes, any intrinsically wrong actions. They hold that any act whatsoever can be justified, given the proper circumstances. This doctrine, appropriately called situation ethics, is an outgrowth of existentialism. Sartre, and existentialists generally, take a completely antinomian attitude toward morality. For them there is no objective moral law; the individual is entirely free to express his own inner attitudes, and when he does, his act has moral value.

Not all situationists go quite this far. Dr. Joseph Fletcher, for example, recognizes the existence of moral standards which are objective and for the most part applicable. He rejects, however, a legalism which would attempt to solve every moral problem in terms of ready-made principles. People are what count, he says, and when the application of a moral principle will do more harm than good, it is not to be applied. Morality, he thinks, can become immoral through overinsistence on principles. People, realizing they have the "freedom to make responsible decisions," should determine whether the principle applies to their case or not.

Thus, though Fletcher holds that adultery is generally wrong because it usually has disastrous effects, yet an occasion might arise where it would do a great deal of good and little or no harm. He gives the case of a certain German woman, imprisoned during World War II in a Soviet concentration camp, who knew that, if she became pregnant, she would be allowed to return to her family. Fletcher suggests she might in good conscience have intercourse with a guard to achieve this worthy purpose.[2] He suggests, too, that abortion might be permissible in the case of a girl who has been raped by a young man who, like herself, is mentally disturbed and a patient at the same sanatorium.[3]

Fletcher would have every situation judged in its own right and a particular solution for it found. Love for the neighbor, not any rigorous insistence upon principle, should dictate the answer to every problem. In his view, "Love is the only norm,"[4] and any act motivated by it is good. Love gives meaning to marriage, he says, and without it sex is nothing but exploitation. Cohabitation by a couple who are in love but cannot marry has, in his opinion, more moral value than a loveless marriage.

CRITIQUE

Situation ethics has quite properly stressed the importance of circumstances as a moral determinant. Traditional moral theory has tended to focus its attention overmuch on the object of the act, forgetting that it is always a case of this person involved in these circumstances at this time. Man must live in a world of everchanging circumstances and it is not always easy for him to see the wisdom of adhering to a principle which seems to benefit no one. And, if primacy is to be given to any one motive, this new approach rightly accords it to love; no man with love in his heart can incur subjective guilt.

Long before the situationists, however, Christianity put a premium on love. The reason Christ gave for Mary Magdalene's sins being forgiven her was that she had loved much. He summed up the entire Mosaic law in the two injunctions: Thou shalt love the Lord thy God above all things and thy neighbor as thyself. What is often forgotten, however, is his other statement: "If you love me, keep my commandments." He left the Ten Commandments intact, and they prohibit blasphemy, murder, theft, lying, and so forth, absolutely and under all and every circumstance.

Situationists reply that terms like *murder* and *theft* are mere abstractions, never verified in the concrete. For them, it is not what is done, but why and in what circumstances one does it, that determines the moral value of the act. When the taking of another's life or property is wrongly motivated, it is immoral, but if done for a proper reason it is a good deed.

Our thought is that these terms can be verified in the objective order. Admittedly, one may kill and not commit murder; there is such a thing as justifiable homicide, as when a person is unjustly attacked and can save his life only by killing the aggressor. It is absurd to hold that the victim loses his right to live in such a case, while the aggressor retains his. Then too, for a killing to be murder, it must be directly intended. A surgeon who, in order to save a woman's life, must excise a cancerous womb which unfortunately contains a living fetus, does not murder the child. He does not operate in order to kill the child although he foresees its death as inevitable. The death of the fetus is only a permitted side effect of the operation. The public executioner is not a murderer, either, even if he unwittingly puts an innocent man to death, for he acts, not on his own authority, but on that of the state.

Murder is the directly intended killing of an innocent person on one's own authority. When all of these elements are found in the act, it is intrinsically evil, immoral under all circumstances. To say that love can justify it is to forget that, for rational beings, reason must guide love. Reason sets bounds to what may be loved and tells us when one love object must yield to another; it sanctions agape, not eros.

When situationists permit direct attacks on fetal life in the name of love, their concept of love is truncated and narrow—it stops at the wall of the womb and ignores the person-to-be resident there. The love which prompts them to relax the laws against divorce is equally shortsighted, since it considers only the husband and wife. It does not concern itself with the children whose proper rearing requires the cooperation of both parents. Neither does it take into account the weakening effect divorce has upon the institution of marriage and this in turn on the stability of peoples and nations.

It appears, too, that the German mother who, in Fletcher's example, gets herself impregnated by the Russian guard, violated the basic principle of the new morality. She used him, treated him as a *thing*, not as a *person*. The couple he speaks of who, though deeply in love, cannot marry but have sexual relations anyway, hardly escape blame, either, even on his own terms. Sexual intercourse is, after all, the most interpersonal of all human relationships. Psychologically, it connotes the complete gift of each to the other, and this inherent symbolism should weigh heavily on all who profess to perform it lovingly. It would seem to require that the partners ratify this unitive symbolism with a juridical bond which makes them forever inseparable. This may appear an excessively legalistic point of view, but the thought occurs: in the end, does it not show more respect for human worth than situationism? It seems to us that, if the nature and meaning of the act by which human life is transmitted is not absolutely to be respected, then it does not mean very much to be a man.

IMMUTABILITY OF THE NATURAL LAW

While man remains man, the essential truth about human nature and the values necessary for proper human living cannot

80

change. Since the natural law is based upon these truths and values, it enjoys the same immutability. As Cicero wrote:

> True law is right reason in agreement with Nature; it is of universal application, unchanging and everlasting; it summons to duty by its commands, and averts from wrong-doing by its prohibitions. ... it is a sin to try to alter this law, nor is it allowable to attempt to repeal any part of it, and it is impossible to abolish it entirely. We cannot be freed from its obligations by Senate or People, and we need not look outside ourselves for an expounder or interpreter of it. And there will not be different laws at Rome and at Athens, or different laws now and in the future, but one eternal and unchangeable law will be valid for all nations and for all times.[5]

St. Thomas held that, though the natural law could be added to "for the benefit of human life,"[6] as happened when men began to wear clothes and enacted laws regulating the ownership of property, the law itself is unchangeable. As a Christian moralist, however, he had to face the fact that God himself appears to have made certain changes in the natural law. He commanded Abraham to kill his son Isaac,[7] ordered the Jews fleeing Egypt to take with them the vessels of their former masters,[8] told Osee to take unto himself a "wife of fornications."[9] This made it seem that there is no natural law properly so-called, that whatever moral law there is has its source more in God's will than in the nature of things.

For St. Thomas, however, nature was always the element determinative of morality. "Whatever is done by God is, in some way, natural," he wrote. All men, whether guilty or not, die the "death of nature," and so "by the command of God, death can be inflicted on any man, guilty or innocent, without any injustice whatever." Then too, "adultery is intercourse with another's wife who is allotted to him by the law emanating from God. Consequently intercourse with any woman, by the command of God is neither adultery nor fornication." "The same," he says, "applies to theft, which is the taking of another's property. For whatever is taken by the command of God, to Whom all things belong, is not taken against the will of its owner, whereas it is in this that theft consists."

St. Thomas' naturalistic approach to morality did not win easy acceptance in his day. In 1277, three years after his death, the bishop of Paris, Stephen Tempier, condemned two hundred and nineteen propositions, among them several held by St. Thomas, and threatened with excommunication anyone who taught them. The voluntaristic position was then considered a more orthodox defense of divine omnipotence; if God is almighty, then he must be able to do anything, even change the fundamental moral law.

Voluntarism was ably espoused by the great Franciscan thinkers, Duns Scotus and William of Ockam. Scotus held that, though reason can indeed recognize that murder and adultery are contrary to man's nature, they are morally wrong only because God has forbidden them.[10] Ockam maintained that God could, by His absolute power, strip adultery, theft, and even blasphemy of their malice and make them meritorious. While he admitted that God's ordered power required Him to operate in accordance with His Sanctity and Wisdom, he still insisted: "It is not because something is right or just that God wills it, but it is right and just because God wills it."[11]

It was in time recognized, however, that God's inability to make square circles, sticks with one end, and rational beings who do right when they act irrationally means nothing more than the incapacity of these things to be. As Grotius wrote:

Measureless as is the power of God, nevertheless it can be said that there are certain things over which that power does not extend. . . . Just as even God cannot cause that two times two should not make four, so He cannot cause that which is intrinsically evil be not evil.[12]

82

This is not to say that voluntarism no longer has its adherents. As we have seen, Kierkegaard interpreted the Abraham-Isaac incident in a voluntarist sense, calling it a "teleological suspension of the ethical." He held that, in order to elicit an act of faith from the patriarch, God suspended the moral law prohibiting murder.[13] And there has recently been a revival of voluntarism by those who, wishing to stand as far apart as possible from Kant's "lay ethics," make God the immediate and unique source of the moral law.

Our view is that this cannot be done without making the moral value of a human act extrinsic and accidental to it, which is not the case. Morality by decree has its place, as when civil authorities make something obligatory which is not so of itself, like paying an income tax or serving in the military. The moral order cannot itself be the product of any fiat, however, divine or human. It is inconceivable that justice, mercy, and charity should lack moral value under any circumstances; their goodness stems from the very nature of things. Between the divine decision to create, which was admittedly free, there stands God's creation, which is the proximate source of the moral law.

Demanding, as it does, that the subject perform the act precisely because God wills it, voluntarism leaves room for morally indifferent acts—those which, though conformed to human nature and therefore not wrong, are yet not done with the explicit intention of doing God's will. It seems better to hold with St. Thomas, however, that, though a human act, taken in the abstract—walking, singing, and so forth—can be morally indifferent, yet when taken in the concrete, all such acts are either morally right or wrong. The natural orientation of the will to good in general guarantees, as he says, a good intention where there is no explicit intention of wrongdoing.[14]

In fact, on the voluntarist premise, it would be impossible for an atheist or an agnostic ever to perform anything but morally indifferent acts. Since they do not acknowledge God's existence, they cannot intend to do His will or violate it. Voluntarists may answer that, since God's existence is so entirely evident, anyone who does not admit it is necessarily in bad faith. There are difficulties connected with this position, however. It is not quite demonstrable, to begin with, that one cannot be a sincere atheist. Karl Marx seems to have been one. It has been said that he was "born" an atheist and "never during the whole course of his life did his conviction undergo the least weakening."[15] Kant, though keenly sensitive to moral obligation, held that God's existence was not philosophically demonstrable. It is not altogether evident, therefore, that atheists and agnostics are necessarily in bad faith, committing what is called the philosophical sin. Indeed, since for voluntarists reason is not the norm of morality, a philosophical sin is not really a moral fault at all. For that, it would have to be theological, a deliberate refusal to do God's will.

We might point out, however, that, in the moral theory we have been proposing, any deliberate refusal to be reasonable, in which philosophical sin consists, at once becomes a moral fault. It is theological because, behind man's rational nature, there stands its Creator whose will is expressed in his creation.

A further weakness in the voluntarist position is its failure to provide a moral norm which is truly ultimate. Its only answer to the question "Why is justice a virtue?" or "Why must I be just?" is "Because God wills it." One may still ask, however, "What difference does that make?" "Why must I do what God wills?" The answer is that it would be unreasonable to disobey the infinitely wise and holy Author of my being. Thus, behind voluntarism's explicit appeal to God's will as the unique source of moral value there is an implicit and ultimate appeal to reason.

CHANGES IN THE NATURAL LAW

Our thesis that the natural law is immutable appears to be contradicted by the fact that certain actions and practices have

84

been approved or at least accepted in one era but rejected as immoral in another. Usury is a case in point. The Mosaic law forbade the Jews to demand any interest on a money loan, and medieval Canon Law continued the prohibition. The thinking was that the practice was contrary to the nature of money. Cows and fruit trees have a natural increase, but not money; its sole purpose was to serve as a medium of exchange. Now, however, the liceity of demanding interest on a money loan is universally unquestioned.

Slavery is another instance of reversible moral attitudes. The great moralists of the past saw nothing inherently wrong with it. For all of his deep insight into man's nature and profound respect for human dignity, Plato condoned the ownership of one person by another, including the right of sale.[16] Not even the fact that the child's father was a freeman or a freedman sufficed to end its servile condition; it remained the property of the mother's master. Aristotle took the same view. "It is clear," he wrote, "that some men are by nature free, and others slaves, and that for these slavery is both expedient and right."[17] Aquinas, with all the benefit of Christian revelation, held the servile state was a condition prescribed for certain people by the jus gentium.[18] Now, however, we consider slavery completely at odds with the nature of man.

Some regard these contradictory attitudes as changes in the natural law itself. Stumpf, for example, takes the diverse judgments on slavery as an indication that "there are no permanent norms of natural law to guide the making of positive laws." He even suggests there is "only one kind of 'law' in the strict sense of the term—the positive law, and it is in connection with the creation of this law that natural law thought emerges." He would in fact have us "abandon the whole idea of natural law and look upon the positive law simply as a set of rules fashioned by each generation to fit its own conception of desirable human behaviour."[19]

Our thought is that leaving each generation free to choose whatever goals it pleases without the controlling influence of a higher law is a sure path to barbarism. Values such as life, liberty, bodily integrity, reputation, and many others, are essential to man regardless of the era or socioeconomic conditions under which he lives. Since the nature of man does not change, what is inconsistent with it at one time will be so at any other. Slavery did not suddenly become immoral in the mid-nineteenth century; it was only then belatedly recognized that man is not a chattel to be owned and dominated by another. The Emancipation Proclamation did not make liberty a human value; it merely gave political recognition to the fact that to be a man is to be, under God, one's own master.

Not all values are mutable, however. Though the nature of man does not change, the nature or function of things can and do. This happened in the case of money. Before the industrial revolution it was merely a medium of exchange, a consumable good; when used, it was used up. It has since become the equivalent of a machine or factory, however, and therefore a capital good. One who lends money now deprives himself of the opportunity to invest it and further enrich himself. This is the title upon which the demand for interest, once termed usury, may now be legitimately based.

Propagation is another value which has undergone change. There was a time when it was greatly to man's benefit to "increase, multiply, fill the earth and subdue it." While national economies were for the most part agricultural and living space plentiful, large families were desirable. Now that all the great nations are highly industrialized, however, the lack of adequate housing and other problems consequent upon the urbanization of society make raising a large family a difficult task and, indeed, undesirable in view of the worldwide population explosion. This situation seems likely to last and while it does, all legitimate efforts to curtail population growth are entirely in order. This, however, is not really a change in the natural law, either, but only in the social and economic conditions to which it is to be applied.

NATURAL RIGHTS

Man's nature is not only the source of law but also of rights. If he has the duty to live, then he must have the right to do so: to make such use of material things as is necessary to sustain his life, defend himself against aggression, and so forth. If, as seems obvious, we are supposed to live in a human way, and certain values, such as liberty, reputation, and property, are necessary for this, then the right to them must be from nature.

The theory of natural rights is an ancient one. Antigone invoked it when she insisted on her right to bury her brother Polyneices despite the prohibition of King Creon. Aristotle approved of her action in terms which show him clearly opposed to the social contract theory later to be espoused by Hobbes and Rousseau. He wrote:

> For there really is, as every one to some extent divines, a natural justice and injustice that is binding on all men, even on those who have no association or covenant with each other.[20]

In the sixth century the natural law theory of rights was incorporated into Justinian's *Code* which, with certain modifications, eventually became the common law of Europe. Out of it developed the European tradition of true liberalism which upheld the rights of the individual vis-à-vis the state. This tradition, vitiated on the Continent through overlong exposure to absolutism, found its way first to England and then to America where it received its finest political expression in the Declaration of Independence. The Founding Fathers knew Locke and through him the political thought of Bellarmine, Suarez, and St. Thomas; many of them were lawyers well versed in English Common Law, and they justified their revolution by appealing beyond statutory law to the law of nature. This, they held, conferred upon men "certain inalienable rights" which it is government's business to defend. Twelve years later, the French revolutionaries invoked that same "higher law," as guarantor of the "natural, inalienable and sacred Rights of man."

The fact that both the American and French revolutionaries based their cases on it is perhaps the best refutation of Kelsen's charge that natural law theory is static, positivism dynamic. As Fuller points out, the opposite is true. Since natural law theory derives the legal order "from certain meaningful notions of justice," and not from any "vacant principle of constitutionalism," it provides the law with an internal principle of growth. In Fuller's judgment, the positivistic notion of law is "about as 'dynamic' as an empty wheelbarrow . . . you can dump anything you wish into it, and you can push it in any direction you like. But it has absolutely nothing to make it go."[21]

The excellence of natural law theory did not prevent its eclipse some two hundred years ago, however, by legal positivism. For positivists there is no higher law, no standard to which enacted law must conform before it becomes law properly so-called. Law is simply what is on the books. For Hobbes, the foremost exponent of positivism, there was no appeal in the matter of law, morality, or rights beyond the "will of the sovereign." He wrote, "Where there is no common power, there is no law; where no law, no injustice."[22] Rousseau held that "The social order is a sacred right which serves as the foundation for all the others."[23]

Karl Marx also adopted a positivistic view of law. For him, law was just an ideology, and there would be no place for it in the classless society. He rejected the concept of natural rights, calling them "liberal illusions."[24] Justice Oliver Wendell Holmes, Jr., late of the United States Supreme Court, held that law was "what the courts do in fact." For him, a person had a right when he fulfilled all the conditions laid down by the state for putting its power on his side. Asked during World War I who was in the right, the Allies or the Central Powers, he answered that it was impossible to tell as yet, since neither side had won. For him, the ultimate arbiter of right and wrong was the strongest nation in the world, since it could coerce the others.

Legal positivism was so much the vogue in pre-Hitler Germany that it was impossible to get a manuscript published if it so much as suggested the existence of a higher law acting as a control over enacted law. The Nazis took full advantage of the situation; since the Reichstag had empowered Hitler to govern by decree, every law of theirs, however iniquitous, was properly enacted. The Nazi experience taught Gustave Radbruch an important lesson on the nature of law. He had previously believed that, in the interest of peace and order, the state had the right to settle authoritatively all disputes among its citizens on matters of value. Life under Hitler convinced him, however, that certain limitations upon governmental power had to exist from the "nature of things." There was, he discovered, such a thing as "lawless law": enactments which, since they do not aim at justice, are not laws at all. He wrote:

> For law, including positive law, cannot be defined otherwise than as an ordering and statute, the meaning of which is to serve justice. Measured by this standard, whole portions of Nationalist Socialist law never attained the level of true law. . . . Because [Hitler] lacked all sense of right he could without a thought enact into law the crudest arbitrariness. . . . we must overcome the positivist legal philosophy which rendered helpless every possible defense against the abuses of Nationalist Socialist legislation.[25]

THE RECENT REVIVAL
OF NATURAL LAW THEORY

The outrages perpetrated by the Nazis, and by the Soviets as well, under the veneer of law have occasioned a modest postwar revival of natural law theory, much of it Kantian in inspiration. Helmut Coing, for example, sees moral obligation originating within the subject himself; the natural law for him is the autonomously known law of personal consciousness, and the supreme ethical values which man discovers within himself are normative for enacted law. For Rudolph Stammler, natural law is a matter of correct thought; it represents oughtness and stands above historical and sociological change.

This return to Kantianism by legal theorists who have recognized the bankruptcy of positivism is a step in the right direction. Kant quite rightly held that the moral law is essentially the law of reason, absolute and immutable. Though for him this law is not natural in the sense that it flows from the nature of man, it is in the sense that it has its basis in our rational nature; for Kant, the *is* of rationality gives rise to the *ought* of morality. Also, Kant's insistence on the dignity of the human person is a consideration which should preclude any totalitarian effort to make him a mere means to the achievement of political goals.

But, though Kantianism has many strong points, it has weak ones, too. Kant's separation of the legal from the moral order is one of them. He defined a right as:

> The conception of the conditions under which the wishes of one man can be reconciled with the wishes of every other man according to a general law of freedom.[26]

This highly technical definition of right might serve as a norm for civil legislators whose function it is to enact laws which will curb license and preserve freedom in the community. But it does not define right as the term is commonly used. People do not apply it only to external actions where there exists the possibility of infringing upon the freedom of others. They use it also in connection with internal actions where no such conflict exists. They say, for example, that a child has a right to the love of its parents, a love which is internal and spiritual. Such love they consider to be the child's due, not because of any positive legis-

90

lation on the subject, but from the nature of things. Nor is there any question here of infringing on the equal freedom of others.

Common usage does not endorse Kant's concept of a right merely as a physical empowerment, either. People regard rights as being primarily moral in character. When they speak of their right to life or liberty, for example, they do not consider it the gift of a benevolent government or as belonging to them only because it can be enforced. Might, in the popular mind, does not make right.

The Thomistic theory of natural law and its corollary, natural rights, is more at one with the popular concept than Kant's. Stumpf rejects it for being too "theological," preferring—incredibly—Hobbes' exposition of it by reason of its "minimal" premises.[27] Actually, St. Thomas' approach is theological only in the sense that, for him, all law began with the Eternal Law. Since God is outside time, the Creative Decree—God's determination to create—was from eternity. It involved no passage from potency to act, no temporal sequence. Since that decree settled upon the existence of certain kinds of being—trees, horses, men —it must also have required that each of these creatures-to-be-in-time should act in accord with its nature. The Creative Decree, in other words, had as its necessary concomitant the Eternal Law. As St. Thomas says:

> Law is nothing else but a dictate of practical reason emanating from the ruler who governs a perfect community. Now it is evident, granted that the world is ruled by divine providence, . . . that the whole community of the universe is governed by the divine reason. Therefore the very notion of the government of things in God, the ruler of the universe, has the nature of a law. And since the divine reason's conception of things is not subject to time, but is eternal . . . therefore it is that this kind of law must be called eternal.[28]

St. Thomas is here talking about the order of being, not the order of knowledge. Logically, law must exist in the mind of the Creator before it can be communicated to the creature, but this does not mean that man must know the law as it is in God before he can know the law of his nature. St. Thomas was perfectly aware that man had no a priori knowledge of God, that whatever knowledge of Him man acquired came from sense experience and was applicable to the Creator only by analogy. For St. Thomas, the natural law was the fruit of reason's reflections on the human situation. He would have found no fault with Grotius' statement that the natural law would retain its validity "even if we should concede that which cannot be conceded without the utmost wickedness, that there is no God, or that the affairs of men are of no concern to Him."[29]

The Thomistic exposition of natural law theory is of such lucidity, consistency, and cogency that it is difficult to see how legal positivism, with its overtones of barbarism and arbitrariness, ever gained ascendancy over it. One recalls in this connection what the great von Jhering, founder of the sociological school of jurisprudence, said on discovering St. Thomas:

> Now that I have come to know this vigorous thinker, I cannot help asking myself how it was possible that truths such as he taught should have been so completely forgotten among our Protestant scholars. What errors could have been avoided if people had kept these doctrines! . . . For my part, if I had known them earlier, I probably would not have written my whole book . . .[30]

Hopefully, then, the present return to natural law theory will not stop at the halfway house of Kantianism, but will go all the way to the mansion of Thomism, its true home.

MORALITY IN PRACTICE

The natural law is promulgated to man through reason. He knows instinctively that reason is his guide to goodness, that for him the injunction "Do good, avoid evil" means "Be reasonable, never unreasonable." He knows that any act which is a denial of the human condition or an attack on a basic human value is irrational and therefore immoral. He realizes that, since he is a man, he ought to act like one—rationally, that is, and in accord with truth.

KNOWLEDGE OF THE NATURAL LAW

The derivation of ought from is, of morality from fact, seems obvious enough. Hume, however, objected to it. He wrote:

> In every system of morality which I have hitherto met with, I have always remarked, that the author proceeds for some time in the ordinary way of reasoning, and establishes the being of a God, or makes observations concerning human affairs; when of a sudden I am surprised to find, that instead of the usual copulations of propositions, *is*, and *is not*, I meet with no proposition that is not connected with an *ought*, or an *ought not*. This change is imperceptible; but is, however, of the last consequence. For as this *ought*, or *ought not*, expresses some new relation or affirmation, it is necessary that it should be observed and explained; and at the same time that a reason should be given, for what seems altogether inconceivable, how this new relation can be a deduction from others, which are entirely different from it.[1]

G. E. Moore sided with Hume on this issue. He labeled the derivation of ought from is the "naturalistic fallacy," and ever since moralists have been going to the most absurd lengths to avoid it. Prichard,[2] for example, holds that "the rightness of an action of a particular kind is absolutely underivative or immediate." Not that the sense of obligation comes out of thin air: facts are needed, but they are amoral; only the perception of obligation represents moral thinking properly so-called. He writes:

> The negative side of all this is, of course, that we do not come to appreciate an obligation by an *argument*, i.e. by a process of non-moral thinking, and that, in particular, we do not do so by an argument of which a premise is the ethical but not moral activity of appreciating the goodness either of the act or of a consequence of the act; i.e. that our sense of the rightness of an act is not a conclusion from our appreciation of the goodness either of it or of anything else.

Philippa Foot, on the other hand, insists that it is neither self-evident nor has it ever been established, by Hume, Moore, or anyone else, that deriving moral conclusions from factual premises is in any way fallacious.[3] She is herself inclined to connect morality with utility, as Bentham did, on the grounds that moral value loses all meaning outside the context of what the act is good for. Schlick is another for whom the naturalistic fallacy held no terror; he related the moral to the useful, defining *good* as that "which is *believed* to bring the greatest happiness."[4] We have already mentioned Toulmin's commonsense observation that people base their moral convictions on reasons which, if challenged, they are prepared to give.[5]

This growing tendency to ignore Moore's cautions against committing the naturalistic fallacy appears to us a return to sanity. If ought is not to be derived from is, how is it to be attained? Moore says that the worthwhileness of certain ends and the duty to perform that act which, among those open to us, will be productive of the most good, is intuited.[6] The trouble is, no one is aware of any such intuition and in any case what is intuited should be a matter of general agreement, which is often not the case with moral judgments. People disagree violently on many moral issues, but not on a proposition such as $2 + 2 = 4$, whose truth the human intellect grasps intuitively.

Our thought is that, though the basic obligation to be reasonable is indeed a matter of intuition for a rational being, the content of moral duty—what is reasonable in the given case—has to be learned from the facts. Would I, by taking this aggressor's life, be playing God? Should I pay this debt when my creditor will use the money to his harm? Ought I keep my promise when I can do more good by breaking it? The practical ought quite evidently derives from the factual is.

St. Thomas held that practical reason, mediating between the individual and reality, easily recognizes what he called the common or first principles of the natural law: that it is wrong to injure people or lie, that it is right to live amicably in society, to restore entrusted property on request, and so forth. In such matters, he held, error was not possible for a person of normal intelligence and experience. When it comes to secondary principles or the application of primary ones, however, mistakes can be made because "The more we descend towards the particular the more frequently we encounter defects."[7] A principle can be generally valid, but inapplicable in a particular case. One ought to return entrusted goods to their owner on demand, for example, but what if he will use them against one's country? Following the principle would then be unreasonable and therefore wrong. St. Thomas says:

> The natural law, as to the first common principles, is the same for all, both as to rectitude and as to knowledge. But as to certain more particular aspects, which are conclusions, as it were, of those common principles, it is the same for all in the majority of cases, both as to rectitude and as to knowledge; and yet in a few cases it may fail, both as to rectitude, by reason of certain obstacles (just as natures subject to generation and corruption fail in some few cases because of some obstacle), and as to knowledge, since in some the reason is perverted by passion or evil habit, or an evil disposition of nature. Thus at one time theft, although it is expressly contrary to the natural law, was not considered wrong among the Germans, as Julius Caesar relates.

St. Thomas saw that people are to some extent the victims of the times in which they live when it comes to discerning the moral law in its fullness. While certain precepts of it are so apparent they cannot be missed, others can be obscured by the dust set up by time and circumstance. He himself, in fact, was to some extent the victim of historical circumstance when he added slavery to his list of additions legitimately made to the natural law "for the benefit of human life."[8] With our greater sensitivity in the area of human rights, we find it hard to see how the Angelic Doctor could have failed to see the immorality of this abominable institution. The fact is, however, that slavery continued to find its defenders, many of them surely in good faith, well into the nineteenth century.

But, though one might include slavery, at least in its more humane and mitigated form, among the secondary precepts of the natural law, infanticide and euthanasia are something else again. These are forms of murder, and their immorality should, one would think, be clear to all. Yet Westermarck, who made an extensive study of the mores of certain primitive people, found infanticide "common among the tribes of North and South America"[9] and he encountered natives who considered it an act of kindness to expedite the death of the aged.[10] His conclusion was that morality is purely subjective and relative. He wrote:

> Men pronounced certain acts to be good or bad on account of the emotions those acts aroused in their minds, just as they called sunshine warm and ice cold on account of certain sensations which they experienced, and as they named a thing pleasant or painful because they felt pleasure or pain. . . . To name an act good or bad ultimately implies that it is apt to give rise to an emotion of approval or disapproval in him who pronounces the judgment. . . . The moral concepts, then, are essentially generalizations of tendencies in certain phenomena to call forth moral emotions.[11]

Westermarck's relegation of moral judgments to the sense order is hardly acceptable, but the problem he proposes must be met. How is it possible for people, however primitive, to commit such egregious moral evils without any awareness at all of wrongdoing? If such acts can be committed in good faith, is there any truth to our thesis that adults with the use of reason are necessarily aware of at least the more general precepts of the moral law?

We believe there is. If these people saw no evil in outright murder or any other obvious violation of the moral law, it would indeed be impossible for us to maintain our thesis. This is not the case, however. There is always some modifying factor, some complicating issue, which makes the given action seem to them a reasonable, and therefore a morally permissible, solution to the problem facing them.

These people know, for example, that they must honor their parents and care for them in their old age. But if their religion teaches that a person's well-being in the next life depends on the strength and vigor he retains on leaving this one, it will seem right to dispatch an aging father or mother before general

97

debility sets in. Again, their acknowledged obligations to their parents may conflict with their duties toward their children. If there is not enough food for all, it will seem reasonable to give it to the young who can perpetuate the tribe and fight for it rather than to the aged who will soon die anyway. Then too, the leader of a nomadic tribe might reasonably judge it justifiable to leave behind a wounded warrior who cannot keep up the pace rather than expose the entire tribe to danger. Indeed, once the liceity of this is settled, a further question occurs. Why not shoot a merciful arrow into a vital spot rather than leave the poor fellow behind to be the prey of wild animals or the sport of pursuing enemies?

What seems to emerge from these grim considerations is that men cannot be expected to know, much less practice, the natural law in its entirety if they are compelled to lead a hand-to-mouth existence with their backs constantly to the wall, insecure and afraid. For this they need civilization and the benefits it brings in the form of law, order, and an abundance, or at least a sufficiency, of this world's goods. Only when people are freed from obsessive concern for their bodily needs can they at last raise their eyes from the furrow and consider what it really means to be a man.

CONSCIENCE

Since our intellects have ready access to the basic truths upon which reasonable action depends, and these truths are for the most part evident, the judgment of conscience will usually be both correct and certain. When it is, it must be obeyed, for if the formal promulgation of the moral law does not exist here, it exists nowhere. Sometimes it will be certain but erroneous, however, as when a person is convinced that a given article, belonging in fact to another, is his. He may follow his conscience and take it. In so doing he does indeed break the law materially but incurs no formal guilt, since conscience is our sole guide in the matter of right and wrong. There are even times when one must follow a conscience which, though erroneous, is certain: when, for example, a citizen is convinced that his country is being attacked and that he must defend it, though in fact it is waging a war of aggression. The authority of conscience loses nothing by reason of the undetected error. A certain conscience, whether correct or erroneous, must be obeyed.

This line of reasoning seems evident enough to the modern mind, but its logic was not always admitted. In the Middle Ages people were expected to conform their views to the teaching of the Church, since it was infallible in matters of faith and morals. Peter Abelard felt the weight of the Church's authority when he was condemned by the Council of Sens in 1140 for holding that the individual was always free to follow the dictates of his own conscience.

St. Thomas did not insist too strongly on the absolute right of the individual to follow his conscience, either. Though he did indeed hold that it was always wrong to go against one's conscience, whether correct or incorrect, he never went so far as to say that it was ever permitted, much less obligatory, to follow an erroneous judgment of conscience. His view was that a man could always consult the proper authorities and have it corrected. Whatever validity there ever was to this view, it is untenable in our present state of religious and philosophical pluralism. A person who, through no fault of his own, is sincerely but erroneously convinced of the rectitude of an action may surely do it.

A doubtful conscience is another matter, however. Here the person is unsure whether, if he acts, he will be doing right or wrong. While his doubt remains, he must not act, for to do so would be to show contempt for the law. If it were to turn out that he in fact violated no law, this would be purely accidental and beside the point; he would still have preferred his own will to the law when he acted. Thus, just as one must always follow a certain conscience, one may never act with a doubtful conscience. These are the two rules of moral action.

One who doubts the permissibility of an action must therefore form his conscience before acting: he must be certain that he is not doing wrong. He must find out what the law is on the matter. If he is making out his income tax report, for example, and fears he may be defrauding the Internal Revenue Department if he fails to report an item of income, he should consult someone who knows the law. In so doing he uses the direct method; he learns the pertinent facts of the case and solves the objective or speculative doubt. He is now objectively certain he is meeting the law's requirements and is doing no wrong.

This is not always possible, however. Sometimes every effort to find out what one's objective obligation is proves unavailing. A businessman may be unable to determine whether he actually owes a sum of money for which he has been sent a bill. A hunter may be unable to decide whether what he has in his gunsight is a man or a deer. Must the businessman pay the alleged debt? May the hunter fire away? Common sense supplies the answer at once. There is no obligation to pay a doubtful debt, but one must not shoot at what may possibly be a human being.

Implicit in these seemingly contradictory solutions is the realization that these are two entirely different categories of doubt. The hunter's problem is not whether he has an obligation to safeguard human life but whether, if he shoots, he will be meeting that obligation. The businessman's concern, on the other hand, is with the very existence of the debt; he wonders whether he has any obligation at all to pay the money. Recognizing the difference between these two kinds of doubt, moralists have formulated two reflex principles which, when properly used, supply the practical certitude which is necessary and sufficient for morally permissible action.

The first of these reflex principles, applicable to the questionable debt and indeed to all cases where the obligation itself is the subject of doubt, is "A doubtful law is no law." The reasonableness of this principle is at once evident. It recognizes that, since obligation by its very nature comes to an antecedently free subject, freedom remains in possession while the case for obligation is doubtful. Applying the principle that there can be no perfection in an effect which is not found in its cause, it refuses to allow premises which are only probable to reach conclusions which are certain.

This first reflex principle seems simple enough in theory, but certain problems arise in applying it. At what point does a law become doubtful and therefore no law? Must the reasons for its nonexistence or nonapplicability in a given case outweigh, or at least equal, those in favor of obligation? Hardly. Doubt arises long before the arguments pro and con are equal. It arises whenever the case for obligation is anything less than certain. As the defenders of probabilism rightly contend, the principle that "A doubtful law is no law" becomes operative as soon as a solidly probable reason can be adduced against the law or in favor of freedom. A debt becomes no debt when there is any good reason to doubt whether it was ever contracted.

The situation is different when the doubt concerns validity, however. Here there is a realized obligation to achieve a certain effect, and the doubt has to do only with whether this means will do the job. In such cases the second reflex principle must be used: "Follow the safer course." One who certainly owes a debt must make sure he pays it, not with money that is probably counterfeit but with valid coin of the realm. One must take every means of safeguarding human life: our hunter must not shoot; a surgeon with a choice of two operational techniques, one which will surely cure the patient and another which will only probably do so, must choose the first.

The kind of certitude required of us before we may act in good conscience must take into account the human condition. It is not necessary to have the same high degree of assurance that the food we are about to eat is not poisoned as we have that the sum of two plus two is four, or that a coin tossed into the air will fall. If we had to have metaphysical or even physical certitude before making practical moral decisions, human affairs would grind to a permanent halt. We would then have to inspect the foundation of every building we enter for fear of needlessly endangering our lives. We would not be able to drive on the highways because we could never rule out the absolute possibility of a serious accident.

As we have said, however, reason is the norm of morality and we are required to refrain from acting only when there is reasonable fear of the untoward. Prudential certitude, which does not rule out the absolute possibility of error, but does eliminate all reasonable or prudent fear of it, is sufficient for morally permissible action. Nothing more is required and nothing less will do.

ON THE FORMATION OF CONSCIENCE

Children are born with no concept of right and wrong. The infant is a complexus of desires whose immediate fulfillment is his sole concern. He soon finds, however, that though some are gratified, others are denied; that, while certain forms of behavior are permitted, even encouraged, others are reproved. When he behaves in one way his mother holds him lovingly and caresses him, her voice soft and assuring. When he behaves in another way she slaps him and her voice takes on a menacing tone. This is strong medicine for a child, for mother is his chief love object and her approval is all-important to him.

Out of such experiences the child learns how he must behave. His moral education has begun, although as yet it hardly deserves to be so-called, his notion of right and wrong being purely external. Right is what he is allowed to do, perhaps rewarded for doing; wrong what he is punished for. The superego conscience is in charge. Its predominating characteristic is anxiety; it is negative, irrational, existing solely on the level of sense. The child is torn between the desire to be himself and the consequences of not being good. He rebels secretly and there is danger here that, if fear remains the only motive for conformity, these rebellious impulses may instill in him an exaggerated sense of guilt which will stay with him all his life. He may develop a puritanical conscience which will regard all pleasure as sinful, all instinctive response suspect.

Because in their case fear at this early stage was not supplemented by love and admiration of their parents, some people never outgrow the superego conscience. The authority of the father or father-substitute, which was meant only as a guide through the prerational period, is internalized in them and they remain subject to its tyranny all their lives. For them morality is a matter of grim duty, self-denial, frustration. Though inwardly they rebel against the unreasonable demands conscience makes upon them, they carefully comply, for the slightest failure to do so occasions unbearable feelings of guilt. They resent the tyranny of the superego conscience, but they cannot contest its authority, and so they are torn apart.

The normal procedure is for the person to pass from superego control to reason control. In the mature adult reason takes over and the person does what is right, not because he has to, but because he wants to. Those elements of the superego conscience which remain no longer oppress the person with guilt feelings based on pure emotion; rather, they present the case for rectitude reflectively and with love. Whatever transgressions occur bring an awareness of objective guilt and perhaps contrition, but not paralyzing self-contempt. The rational or, as Fromm calls it, the "humanistic" conscience is the person's own voice, the voice of reason, not that of external authority threatening punishment or promising reward. The person who has it is free and does not fear his freedom. He is captain of his soul.

Parents can be of great assistance in helping their children form a rational conscience. They can, by their example, point the way to a truly objective value system. They can, as soon as the child is ready for it, make it clear to him that the action is not just forbidden but wrong, and for these reasons.

SCRUPULOSITY

Parents are only human, however, and there will always be people who fail to develop into mature adults. There will always be perfectionists, ever unhappily aware of the yawning gap between the sorry performance which represents the best they can do and the ideal which authority requires them to meet. Among such aberrant people, the best known to moralists is the scrupulous person: the one who torments himself by reviewing over and over again past improprieties that were best forgotten. The more severe cases require medical and psychiatric treatment, but the less seriously afflicted can be helped if they will place themselves in the hands of some wise and prudent counselor. They must follow his direction blindly, ignoring the thousand and one doubts that plague them. It may sound strange, to say that one person should surrender his power of self-direction to another, but in this case it is the only reasonable thing to do, since the scrupulant is incapable of self-direction.

Though the scrupulous person must be led by the hand like a child at first, he should be encouraged to make his own decisions, to exercise himself in conscious deliberation and responsible choice. This will develop in him an awareness of his power of self-direction and help him to mature. The realization that only prudential certitude is required of him will help reduce the agony of decision-making. Scrupulosity may not be fully cured by these measures, but it can be controlled so as to allow the scrupulant to function effectively as a human being.

104

THE PRINCIPLE OF THE DOUBLE EFFECT

We are sometimes confronted with actions which, if performed, will, beside the good we intend, also do harm. The surgeon, for example, if he excises the cancerous womb will also kill the fetus it contains. The fireman cannot save the child without getting himself hurt, perhaps killed. The country cannot be defended without risking the lives of its young men. To kill Antiochus, Eleazar had to slash the belly of the elephant on which the king was riding, which meant bringing the huge animal down on top of him.[12] May such actions, productive of two effects, one good, one evil, be performed?

Instinctive common sense assures us they may, but moralists struggled long and hard to elaborate the theoretical justification of such actions. St. Thomas set down its essentials when dealing with the requisites for blameless self-defense. He maintained—overrigorously, we think—that, though the victim might kill the aggressor if necessary, he must not intend to do so; death had to be the unintended effect of efforts directed only at saving one's own life.[13] Scholastic moralists in the sixteenth and seventeenth centuries further developed the theory and in modern times Jean Pierre Gury, the great Jesuit moralist, explained it with full lucidity and applied it to the whole area of morality. Called the principle of double effect, it stipulates that four conditions must be fulfilled for the action to be licit.

First, the action itself must not be immoral: evil, that is, by reason of its object, or what is done. Since the end does not justify the means, actions like murder and theft simply may not be performed, regardless of how much anyone benefits from them.

Second, the good effect must not be brought about by means of the evil one. If it is, then evil is directly intended as a means to an end. This, as we see it, is what makes it wrong for a captured spy to swallow the vial of cyanide his superiors have provided him with for just such a contingency. Even if one transmits the debatable question whether it is ever permissible to swallow a lethal dose of poison, the difficulty still remains that the only direct effect of swallowing it is death. Suicide, a moral evil, then becomes the means by which the spy protects his country.

This second requirement of the double effect principle also creates a problem with regard to the liceity of performing a hysterectomy on a woman who, the doctor says, will not survive another pregnancy. The threat to her life does not come from the condition of the womb precisely, but rather from a possible future pregnancy; if this is avoided, there will be no problem at all. There seems to be no justification, then, for excising the womb.

There are difficult problems in this area, however, which we do not pretend to solve. For example, this same argument, that it is illicit to excise an organ which is no threat to the person's life, can also be used against allowing the donation of a healthy kidney to one's twin brother. However charitably motivated, the act is vitiated at the start, it would appear, by the unjustified excision.

The intuition that such a donation is not only licit but laudable has led moralists to look beyond the principle of totality, which justifies operations necessary to save a person's life, to the principle of solidarity, which views mankind as being in a way one and permits the donation of a healthy surplus organ to another who is in need of it. If one may give one's life for the neighbor, they reason, why not a kidney?

A further development in this area is the growing tendency to regard the various steps in such actions—the excision of the donor's kidney, say, and its implantation in the donee—not in a means-end relationship, but as constituting one moral unit, justified in its totality by the ultimate good intention. Might not the Pill, for example, be used to sterilize a woman who, because of her morbid fear of becoming pregnant again, cannot be a proper wife or mother? We mean temporarily, of course, long enough for a psychiatrist to treat her and hopefully restore her to normalcy.

Third, the action must not be performed in order to bring about the evil effect. If it is, then evil is directly intended. A doctor, for example, might perform a perfectly licit hysterectomy but for a wrong reason; not to save the woman's life but to kill the fetus contained in the cancerous womb. Or, in war, a bombardier might direct explosives at a legitimate military target, but in the hope of killing some civilian enemy of his living in the target area.

Fourth, there must be a proportion between the two effects. To do a little good, one is hardly justified in causing a great evil. The police, for example, may not, in order to prevent a criminal from escaping, shoot indiscriminately into a crowd.

When these four requisites of the double effect are fulfilled, the act is licit. The victim of a rape attack may leap from a high cliff to certain death in defense of her virginity. A surgeon may excise a cancerous womb even though it contains an inviable fetus, provided the operation is necessary to save the woman's life. Soldiers pursued by the enemy may drive their jeep down a narrow alley which offers the only avenue of escape, even though it means running down an innocent civilian. An Alpine guide, himself securely dug in on one side of a deep crevasse, but whose party is hanging down along the length of the guide rope—there being no possibility of his hauling them up or of their being rescued in time—may cut the rope.

A nation has the right to defend its sovereignty and territorial integrity by war if necessary, and in the course of it munition factories may be bombed, even though this causes some incidental damage to nonmilitary property and the deaths of some noncombatants. Modern warfare may involve the use of thermonuclear weapons, however, and here the problem of proportion comes in. The devastation they inflict may easily exceed the good which prompts their use.

LAW AND MORALITY

Though James and Dewey held otherwise, morality is in fact to some extent individual. A man has certain duties-to-self and would have them even if he were the only human being alive, with no other to share his moral solitude. The solitary thinker would indeed have no opportunity to lie or oppress his neighbor, but it would still be wrong for him to commit suicide.

THE STATE: A NATURAL SOCIETY

Morality is also, and more importantly, social in character, however. As Rousseau said:

> Society must be studied in the individual and the individual in so-
> ciety; those who desire to treat politics and morals apart from one
> another will never understand either.[1]

It is in fact questionable whether a man could long survive in
isolation from his fellows, much less develop his potentialities
to any satisfactory degree. Human nature is inherently social;
man is meant to live in the company of others. Why else, as
Aristotle argued, would nature have equipped him with the faculty of speech?

Aristotle saw man as ordered by nature to the formation of
certain definite societies.[2] The first and most basic of these was
marriage, which he describes as a "union of those who cannot
exist without each other . . . not formed of deliberate purpose."
Out of it, through the impulse of nature, comes the family.
Much that is necessary for the fully human life lies outside the
reach of the isolated family, however. For this reason, and also
because sexuality is naturally exogamous, families tend to unite
and to form villages. The process goes on:

> When several villages are united in a single complete community,
> large enough to be nearly or quite self-sufficing, the state comes
> into existence, originating in the bare needs of life, and continu-
> ing in existence for the sake of a good life. And therefore, if the
> earlier forms of society are natural, so is the state, for it is the
> end of them, and the nature of a thing is its end. For what each
> thing is when fully developed, we call its nature, whether we are
> speaking of a man, a horse, or a family. Besides, the final cause
> and end of a thing is the best, and to be self-sufficing is the end
> and the best.

Thus, for Aristotle, the state was a natural society. Any being
able to live a decent life apart from it had to be either a "beast
or a god"; it could not be a man because man was "by nature a
political animal."

Aristotle's *Politics* was unfortunately not available to the
Fathers of the Church. Even had it been, they would perhaps not
have shared his view that the state was a natural society. The

Roman Empire was so thoroughly pagan in organization and spirit that they could hardly have seen it otherwise than as the work of sin. St. Augustine read great significance into the scriptural statement that Cain the fratricide built the first city, while his more virtuous brother Abel was content to be merely a "sojourner on earth."[3] He recommended that Christians concern themselves with the celestial city which was to be their eternal home rather than the city of man.

By the thirteenth century political augustinism was no longer an acceptable or even possible attitude, however. Europe had in the meantime evolved into Christendom and its people could hardly place their baptized princes in the same category as Nero and Diocletian. The medieval Christian was as proud of his city as any Greek had ever been of Athens or Sparta. With its soaring cathedral and religious shrines it appeared more a monument to the faith than the work of sin.

Fortunately at this juncture the missing works of Aristotle made their appearance from across the Pyrenees, and in his *Politics* scholars found ample justification for the new prideful attitude of Christians toward their cities. St. Thomas, who saw so much that was true and valid in the works of the philosopher, ratified the Aristotelian thesis that the state is a natural society. Men, he held, never outgrow their need for the instruction, counsel, and good example of their fellows. The life of solitude might do for a perfect man like John the Baptist, but it was "fraught with very great danger" for the vast majority.[4] He went on to baptize Aristotle's thesis, holding that political society would have existed even if man had not fallen from the state of original innocence. And in such a society of the unfallen there would have been authoritative direction, too, because "a social life cannot exist among a number of people unless under the presidency of one to look after the common good."[5]

Hobbes and Rousseau rejected this teaching on the natural sociability of man and its inevitable actuation in the state. For them political society was merely a de facto, not a de jure institution; it owed more to historical accident than to the nature of things. Hobbes attributed its origin to egotism and fear rather than to man's instinctive love of his fellowman and his natural desire to cooperate with others for the good of all. Having observed the disregard his countrymen exhibited for the common welfare during the 1642-1649 Civil War in England, he generalized upon the experience and reached the conclusion that man was inherently antisocial and self-regarding, a wolf to his neighbor. The "state of nature," by which he meant the human condition without the state, was in his view a "war of all against all." No one was safe, either in his property or his person and, to end this intolerable situation, people formed the state. Distrusting and fearing one another, they entered into the social contract and granted the sovereign absolute power to govern them.[6]

For Rousseau, man was *extra*social rather than *anti*social. He had no need of his fellows, but felt no antipathy toward them, either.[7] Man, he held, had once lived like an animal: wandering through the woods, without reason or speech, following his naturally good instincts, communing with nature, alone and self-sufficient. Only in a later stage did he begin to associate with others of his kind, learn to speak, marry, and lead a primitive kind of family life which left him free to leave his mate at will.

A third stage followed, in which man discovered certain arts and acquired some rudimentary scientific knowledge. Private ownership was introduced and along with it came quarrels, even war. For the sake of peace and security, men entered into the social contract. While Rousseau got the basic idea of this from Hobbes, his conception of it is somewhat different. Hobbes' "sovereign" is very definitely "other," an authoritarian figure to be obeyed without question. Rousseau, however, held that in the social contract one did not give oneself to any single person, but to the totality.

The advantage of this, in Rousseau's view, was that "each, giving himself to all, gives himself to nobody; and as there is not one associate over whom we do not acquire the same rights which we concede to him over ourselves, we gain the equivalent of all that we lose, and more power to preserve what we had." On entering into the contract, the individual does indeed lose his own unlimited natural liberty, but he gains civil liberty, which consists in obedience to the general will. Since this is, or at least should be a projection of his own will, in obeying it he really obeys himself.

We find the Aristotelic-Thomistic concept of the state as a natural society vastly preferable to the social contract theory of Hobbes and Rousseau. While man's nature does not physically force him to live in society, as instinct compels wolves to travel in packs, for example, it does morally necessitate his doing so. He naturally seeks the company of his fellowman, feels the need of communicating with him and seeking his advice when he is perplexed. He needs others to teach him the accumulated knowledge of the past; only so can mankind push on and gain that mastery of the arts and sciences which makes for the truly human life. When men live in society, they can draw upon one another's genius and learning: the architect upon the engineer, so that gradually the City emerges with its aqueducts and bridges, its ordered streets and tranquil homes—a fitting place for human habitation.

HEGEL ON THE STATE

Hegel is remarkable for his admiration of the state.[8] It was for him the most complete expression of man's rationality, and one could not be truly human or free outside of it. As a consequence, he wrote:

> Since the State is mind objectified, it is only as one of its members that the individual himself has objectivity, genuine individuality, and an ethical life.

112

Individual heroism had its place in Hegel's view; he saw the need of it where law and order did not exist, as on our Western frontier, but he distrusted its very individuality. He much preferred the well-regulated, orderly life of the state, where among citizens "the habitual practice of ethical living appears as second nature." The "ethical" for him was in fact synonomous with the "customary" (*das Sittliche*); here, he felt, was "mind living and present as a world."

There is in Hegel a tendency to conceive the state in terms of totalitarian absolutism. This in his political theory once made him the darling of the Prussian Court and, more recently, caused both National Socialism and communism to look to him for ideological support. This view of the relationship between man and the state is of course incorrect. The human person is an absolute where other men or organizations are concerned. He is not a mere means by which the state achieves its ends. The state is rather a means by which he seeks fulfillment. But then, at least in his mature age, Hegel realized all this; though the state remained for him the culmination of man's ethical life, he recognized that there were certain human values—art, religion, and philosophy—which can hardly be secured without society and the freedom it ensures, and do transcend it.

It would seem, then, that for Hegel the state, for all its excellence, remained essentially a means of securing those goods which pertain most significantly to the perfection of man. He cannot be claimed, therefore, as a sponsor for totalitarian doctrines which admit of no value above society and subordinate man in his every aspect to the social good. His political theory, we rather think, deserves a better fate. He is particularly to be commended for making the state the product of reason.

THE NEED FOR LAW

Political society makes it possible for man to live a truly human life by maintaining public order, protecting property,

113

enforcing contracts, and so forth. It does this through law, the need for which in the regulation of human affairs has been generally recognized. St. Thomas, as we have seen, held there would have been authoritative direction through law, even had the human race persevered in the state of original innocence. Not all philosophers are in agreement with him however.

Karl Marx, for example, considered law an ideology, a reflection of the way men are in fact related to one another in the production of goods under capitalism, but doomed to disappear under communism.[9] While private ownership is allowed to continue, he held, the economically dominant class necessarily thinks in terms of mine and thine. Left no alternative by economic forces, they enact laws against stealing and all the other capitalistic vices in order to protect their property and preserve the status quo. There is no point in criticizing these laws; they are neither right nor wrong, but simply mirror the economic situation in a purely mechanical way. Indeed, for Marx, morality was just another ideology, bound to disappear along with law, the state, and the rest of the superstructure once the common ownership of property is introduced.

We have already mentioned, in our critique of Marxist moral theory, the unhappy situation consequent upon the Communist party's attempt to do without law immediately after the 1917 Revolution in Russia. This experience convinced the Soviet authorities of the need for law, and they reinstated it in 1922. Pashukanis' thesis—that, since law would inevitably disappear in the propertyless society, there could not be a truly Marxist theory of law—was discarded. However orthodox it may have been, it tended to create disrespect for law and, at least until Ivan was fully communized, law there had to be.

Vishinsky has since come forward with justification of a sort for the revival of law in the Soviet Union. The new law, he says, expresses the will of the worker; it embodies the social

114

gains made since the Revolution and aims at extirpating the capitalistic spirit by properly relating people to one another in the production of goods. Since it promotes the ongoing Revolution, it is the ideal law, the law that ought-to-be, and Ivan should obey it mainly because of its moral content.

It seems strange that the Soviets, materialists that they are, should stress so strongly the moral content of their law and the obligation it imposes on the citizen's conscience. One wonders what has happened to Marx's dismissal of the moral point of view as unscientific and to Lenin's contention that the dictatorship of the proletariat is ultimately based on force, not law.

The agonizing Soviet encounter with domestic law had its counterpart on the international scene.[10] Here again, their first approach followed the orthodox Marxist thesis that there was no such thing as international law. How could there be when the Revolution was supposed to be worldwide, bringing down the apparatus of state everywhere? Also, law was by its very nature the product of the economically dominant class, and no such class existed on the international level, every nation being composed of rich and poor alike.

Theory had to yield to fact, however. Revolution or no, states continued to exist and the Soviet Union had to deal with them. Korovin, the legal realist, was now ready to admit that international law did indeed exist. He insisted, however, that it was merely the product of agreement among absolutely sovereign nations. There was, he held, no higher law determining what could be agreed upon or requiring that agreements, once made, be kept.

The realist stage is now passé. Soviet lawyers are presently espousing a doctrine which sounds very much like traditional natural law theory. Shursholov, for example, holds that, to be valid, a treaty must conform to certain general principles: it must promote universal peace and the security of nations, show proper regard for national sovereignty, territorial integrity, and so forth. These principles, it would appear, transcend positive law and are normative for international relations.

The Soviet experience with law, starting with utter rejection of even positive law and ending with unabashed acceptance of natural law theory, carries a lesson for antinomians. While man is indeed inherently social, he is not always willing to subordinate his individual interests to the common good. Some people need to be coerced practically all the time, and even the generally well-disposed profit from the no-nonsense directives and sanctions laid down by law.

Lon Fuller suggests that law to a great extent shapes the moral attitudes of the community—a man drives his car carefully, he says, not so much because of his concern for human life but because the highway police have formed his conscience.[11] In this he echoes Aristotle's contention that "lawgivers make men good by habituating them to good works." St. Thomas had the same thought:

> . . . man has a natural aptitude for virtue; but the perfection of virtue must be acquired by man by means of some kind of training. . . . But since some are found to be depraved . . . it was necessary for such to be restrained from evil by force and fear, in order that, at least, they might desist from evil-doing, and leave others in peace, and that they themselves, by being habituated in this way, might be brought to do willingly what hitherto they did from fear, and thus become virtuous. Now this kind of training, which compels through fear of punishment, is the discipline of laws.[12]

LAW AND CONSCIENCE

Though coercion is, at least in man's present imperfect condition, a necessary feature of law, it is not the essential constituent of law. Law cannot be, for rational beings, simply what they will be punished for transgressing. It is not, as the positivists contend, simply what is on the books, with the will of the sovereign lending it authority. St. Thomas defined law more properly as "an ordinance of reason for the common good, promulgated by him who has care of the community."[13]

People do not form states, after all, in order to obey the arbitrary whims of any ruler, but for their own advancement, convenience, and happiness. They recognize with St. Thomas that "a tyrannical law, through not being according to reason, is not a law . . . but a perversion of law."[14] When legitimate authority enacts a law properly so-called, one that is necessary or at least useful for the common good (protective, that is, of some acknowledged value), citizens generally recognize their obligation to abide by it. Not precisely or merely because they might otherwise be caught and punished—an attitude more animalistic and childish than human and adult—but as a matter of conscience. With St. Thomas they realize that:

> Laws framed by men are either just or unjust. If they be just, they have the power of obliging in conscience, from the eternal law whence they are derived, according to *Prov.* viii, 15: "By Me kings reign, and lawgivers decree just things."[15]

Dr. Stumpf is of the opinion that the act prescribed by law is morally obligatory even before it is made legally binding. This is often true. No civil legislation was needed to make it wrong to exploit working people by paying them mere subsistence wages. This is wrong in itself, and laws prohibiting it are merely declarative of moral obligation. For those who are unaware of the inherent immorality of the practice, they make it known and add a sanction in the form of a fine or imprisonment.

This is not always the case, however. One might say that, since the state is a natural society, needed for man's full development, there is an obligation for its members to support it. Nature does not specify any particular means of doing so, however; it might be done by voluntary contributions or in some other way. Congress has settled on the income tax as the most efficient solution to the problem. Since the Income Tax Law tends to promote the common good, it binds in conscience; it is constitutive, not merely declarative, of moral obligation.

MORALITY THE MATRIX OF LAW

Law epitomizes the moral convictions of the community. When enough people become convinced that a given practice is wrong, a law is soon enacted prohibiting it. Such a consensus is often long in the making. It took almost a hundred years of our existence as a nation before the inhumanity of slavery was generally enough recognized to make emancipation possible, and even then the effort almost tore our nation apart.

Having received a strong infusion of morality in the process of enactment, law receives another as it is enforced in the courts. The judge, called upon to enforce what Professor Hart has termed the penumbra of the law—that area lying outside its core, where its meaning is unclear—must reach beyond strict legality and draw upon moral principles. He decides the case in terms of what is fair or equitable. His decision expresses the as yet unformulated sentiment of the community, making jural what was before merely implicit in the law. His decision does not so much change the law-that-is or add to it externally as make it grow through the inner dynamism of reason in the direction of the ought-to-be. Thus the morally sensitive judge avoids turnstile justice, which may easily prove to be injustice.

Instances of such judicial lawmaking on the basis of moral conviction abound. In 1889, the New York Court of Appeals was called upon to decide whether a boy who had killed his grandfather to make sure the old gentleman did not carry out his threat to disinherit him should be disqualified as an heir. The court held he should, basing its judgment on the principle that no one should be allowed to profit by reason of crime. The principle enjoyed no legal sanction; it was drawn from the realm of the right and just. To make it decisive in the case, the judges had to set aside a legally valid will and, in effect, write a new one on the basis of what the deceased would have done if . . .[16]

Again, the law on manslaughter is quite clear in general, but cases often arise requiring an estimate of the degree of moral fault involved. In 1842, for example, a United States Circuit Court tried the case of a seaman named Holmes who had, with the help of several other crew members, tossed sixteen people, all passengers, out of a sinking lifeboat. His defense was that he had done it under orders, having already once refused to obey the mate's command that he do so; that the boat would otherwise have sunk with all aboard; that any duty he had to protect the passengers by reason of his official position was nullified by the stressful circumstances which left only the law of self-preservation in force. The court, uncertain as to the full extent of the fellow's moral guilt, tempered the law with mercy. Empowered to fine him $1,000 and to imprison him for three years, it fined him only $20 and sentenced him to six months of solitary confinement at hard labor.[17]

Some of our modern justices are quite frank about their reliance on moral principle in interpreting and applying the law-that-is. Mr. Justice Cardozo, who once remarked that "Much of our law is judge-made, and there are those who think it is the best," often found moral considerations decisive. "The scope of legal duty," he wrote, "has expanded in obedience to the urge of morals." And again: "What we are seeking is not merely the justice that one receives when his rights and duties are determined by the law as it is; what we are seeking is the justice to which the law in its making should conform."[18]

This point of view forces itself particularly upon judges who sit in appellate courts, sometimes in opposition to their avowed principles. There was no jurist more professedly opposed to the mingling of law and morality than Mr. Justice Holmes. Anyone who looked to moral principles—if indeed there were any, which he doubted—for the source of law was looking in the wrong place. There was no higher law exercising control over enacted law. Law was simply "what the courts do in fact," and the United States Supreme Court, through its power of judicial review, was the ultimate sovereign in the land. His concept of law was so completely positivistic that he professed to hear, even in the common law, the "articulate voice of a sovereign who could be identified." Yet, in *McDonald v. Mabee*, he held that no judgment should ever be contrary to natural justice and that no legal fiction should ever be allowed to deny fair play. Neither of these concepts, it need hardly be pointed out, enjoy constitutional endorsement, but they do strongly suggest moral norms.

Mr. Justice Black also professedly opposed the intrusion of moral principles into the law. In *United States v. Bethlehem Steel*, for example, he considered the moral element irrelevant. It might well be, as Frankfurter maintained, "contrary to moral and equitable principles" for a company to make a twenty-two percent profit on a shipbuilding contract, particularly when the government guaranteed it against loss, but that did not make it illegal. It was up to Congress, Black held, not the court, to enact laws against war profiteering. For judges to "rest their interpretation of statutes on nothing but their own conceptions of 'morals' and 'ethics,'" he wrote in his dissent to the *Mercoid* decision, was "dangerous business." And yet, in *Muschany v. United States*, Black's dissenting opinion recommended that the case be remanded to the Circuit Court for it to pass on the issues of "fraud, unconscionable dealing and unjust enrichment."

These instances illustrate how law, having received in the very process of enactment an infusion of morality which not even a morally neutral judge can ignore, is steered still further in the direction of the ought-to-be by judges sensitive to moral norms. As Dr. Stumpf has well said, "Law moves in a strange and imprecise way between the domain of power and morality."

LAW AND THE COMMON GOOD

Since law is the product of the community's moral insights, and these vary all the way from near-blindness to full vision, the legal process is a matter of growth and development, trial and error. No human legislator has that complete knowledge of the Good in all its transcendence which Plato required of his philosopher-king. No man or human assembly is privy to any Ideal Law that will solve every social issue once and for all. Legislatures may adjourn, but they can never disband. New social problems arise constantly and lawmakers must face them patiently and pragmatically, settling for what is possible here and now, always being careful not to get ahead—or, at least, not too far ahead—of the moral commitment of the people.

William James made some shrewd observations on this point, some of which we discussed earlier.[19] He would have the philosopher cherish no absolutes, champion no fixed set of values or ideals, but be ready to opt this way or the other in accordance with popular demand. Not that he should stand idly by while the very foundations of society are being swept away. No, since every change involves a certain amount of danger, he should favor those demands which will "prevail at the least cost" and "destroy the least possible number of other ideals." "The philosopher must be a conservative," James cautioned, "and in the construction of his casuistic scale must put the things most in accordance with the customs of the community on top." Though he yields to the new when necessary, he holds on to the traditional when possible. In this way he brings about a social equilibrium more or less acceptable to both sides of the controversy under review.

No law or custom is ever acceptable to all in the community, James held. The rich may be greatly in favor of private ownership and the laws forbidding theft, but the poor are oppressed by them. Laws prohibiting divorce and prescribing monogamy please the majority, but they inhibit those who would prefer to be sexually free. James wrote:

> See our kindliness for the humble and the outcast, how it wars with that stern weeding-out which until now has been the condition of every perfection in the breed. . . . The pinch is always there . . . [there is always a] rumbling and grumbling in the background. . . . [Just as] our present laws and customs have fought and conquered other past ones, so they will in their turn be overthrown by any newly discovered order which will hush up the complaints that they still give rise to, without producing others louder still.

James' thesis seems at first to be entirely too relativistic, but with certain emendations it is acceptable. One would wish that he had addressed himself to the legislator, not the philosopher. Whatever the philosopher's concern for the concrete situation to which they are applied, he must hold on to moral absolutes. Legislators, however, must be sensitive to public opinion and representative of it. No democratic government can oppose the will of its people, and an elected official who does not respond to the views of his constituency will not remain in office for very long.

This means that legislators must take into account the cultural and moral limitations of the people and not enact laws simply because they are ideal or ought to be on the books. Perhaps the Eighteenth Amendment was nobly motivated, but the people were not prepared to be quite that abstemious. It was unenforceable and served only to create disrespect for law.

Recognizing that it cannot fight its people, a government may wisely decide to tolerate a practice which, though morally reprehensible, does not have too adverse an affect upon social living, rather than produce greater public disturbance by attempting to stop it. St. Thomas asks himself the question "Whether it belongs to the human law to repress all vices?" and answers in the negative:

122

. . . laws imposed upon men should be in keeping with their condition . . . human law is framed for a number of human beings, the majority of whom are not perfect in virtue. Wherefore human laws do not forbid all vices, from which the virtuous abstain, but only the more grievous vices, from which it is possible for the majority to abstain; and chiefly those that are to the hurt of others, without the prohibition of which human society could not be maintained; thus human law prohibits murder, theft and such-like.[20]

The moral views of the American people were strong enough in 1879 to outlaw polygamy among the Mormons, and on some issues touching morality the public consensus in our country has grown with the passage of years. The fact that human dignity does not depend on race or color, for example, has become apparent to the vast majority of Americans, so that they recognize the wrongness of discrimination on any such basis. It will take some time yet to end segregation in schools throughout the land and to eliminate all forms of discrimination in housing and employment, but the way is clear and we have already gone a long way.

On some other moral issues the consensus which our nation once had has been eroded. In many states there once were laws forbidding the sale of contraceptives and allowing divorce and abortion only in the most extreme circumstances. These have either been rescinded or are presently being challenged as relics of a morality that is passé. The problem arises: must the lawmaker who believes in traditional morality follow his conscience and resist what he considers the legalizing of immorality or may he, as James suggests, simply follow the principle of majority, or vocal minority, rule?

Our view is that he should follow a middle course. Surely he must not, on the one hand, attempt to enact laws simply because they represent his own moral convictions or those of his Church. But neither may he, on the other, throw moral standards to the wind and make the will of the majority his only norm.

Though there are indeed issues on which he may in conscience yield to the popular will, there are others on which he must follow his own convictions.

Let us say our legislator considers contraception immoral. The argument against it from the natural law is actually quite strong; the sexual act is essentially generative, and to deliberately render it sterile means violating nature's prescription with regard to its proper use. The trouble is, though, that many, perhaps most, of our people do not see the force of this reasoning. They see no evil in frustrating nature. After all, do we not pare our nails, thus frustrating nature's attempt to make them grow long? And reroute rivers in opposition to the way nature dictates that they go? And, indeed, how can the sexual act be essentially or primarily generative when most such acts do not achieve conception at all?

Our legislator may not be much impressed with these attempts to refute the natural law argument against contraception, but many people consider them unanswerable. Indeed, some prefer not to enter into any theoretical discussion of the matter at all. Contraception is the only practical solution to their own personal marital problems, and that is the end of it. Many see it as a sensible and effective way of solving the worldwide population explosion and therefore as morally permissible.

It would be highly imprudent for a legislator to insist on enacting or retaining a law forbidding the sale of contraceptives in a community where this kind of thinking prevails. The law could not be enforced and would serve only to promote disrespect for law in general. Here the legislator may and should yield to popular pressure.

The same reasoning, mutatis mutandis, applies to divorce. Here again our legislator may be convinced that no human authority can break the marriage bond and allow remarriage. Arguing from the nature of the sexual act and the psychological attitude which ought to characterize a rational being's performance of it, he may have reached the conclusion that it is only for the totally committed, those who have given themselves to one another for life. His conviction will, however, run counter to the view held by many, that only love justifies marriage, that when it ceases the marriage should be terminated, that when a mistake has been made in the choice of a partner, it should be rectified, and so forth.

Our thought is that here again public authorities are entirely justified in yielding to the community viewpoint. They may in good conscience grant legal relief to the considerable portion of the population who believe that divorce should be granted for such reasons as infidelity, desertion, extreme cruelty, and the like. Those who see validity in the natural law argument against divorce or wish to follow their Church's teaching that the state has no power over the marriage bond need not avail themselves of the legal right. But they cannot expect the state to impose their views on the community as a whole.

Of late there has been a great deal of social pressure put upon legislators to ease the antiabortion laws, even to the point of allowing abortion-on-demand. The problem arises: may our legislator, if he is himself convinced that abortion is an unjustified attack on an innocent human being, approve such legislation? Our view is that he may not. There are limits to the principle of majority, or vocal minority, rule. There are issues on which legislators must take a stand, and the inviolability of innocent human life is one of them.

Some would say that the fetus is not innocent at all, that it is an unjust aggressor against the woman's life or, perhaps, against the welfare of the children already born. It is difficult to see, however, how a fetus who has been brought into existence by the free action of its parents and who is merely developing as nature intends can be labeled an unjust aggressor.

Others would say the fetus is not human, that it is just a blob of protoplasm, measuring only two inches as late as eleven weeks after conception, that it is not a person and has no rights. This argument is of no use to those who claim that fetal life is not new but is continuous with that of the parental spermatazoon and ovum. If life no longer begins but only began, once and for all, in the remote past when animate cells emerged from the primeval slime, and now is merely passed on like the flame from a torch, then it is as much to be respected in the newly conceived zygote as in an adult. Since for the abiogenist size or stage of development is not the issue, but only life itself, abortion takes on all the malice of murder.

For those who recognize the rather obvious fact that the life of the fetus is not that of the parental spermatazoon or ovum, but something entirely new and original, the issue is somewhat more complex. There at once arises the problem whether this life is truly human from the moment of conception or whether it becomes so in the course of its development. Aristotle held the latter view and sanctioned early abortion.[21] Aquinas also held that a certain amount of development and growth was needed before the fetus acquired a human soul. He did not, however, concede that abortion, even in the earliest stage, was licit.[22] One does not, after all, carelessly kill what may very well be a human being; one follows the safer course.

Some doctors would place the beginning of human life in the fetus as early as the blastocyst stage, which starts within two weeks after conception. There is by then sufficient differentiation to distinguish it from any nonhuman species, they argue, and from then on neither twinning nor recombination occur: the blastocyst, implanted in the uterine cavity, needs only to grow in order to become one of us.[23]

Medical testimony to this effect should give pause to a legislator who contemplates yielding to social pressure to have the antiabortion laws liberalized. The purpose of law is to defend the right to life, not deny it. Radbruch well remarked, there is such a thing as "lawless law."

126

NOTES

CHAPTER I

1 Cf. B. Spinoza, *Letter* 58.
2 B. Spinoza, *Ethics*, P. V, prop. 2, note.
3 David Hume, *Treatise on the Correction of the Understanding*, 2, 13.
4 David Hume, *Treatise of Human Nature*, edited by L. A. Selby-Bigge. Fair Lawn, N. J.: Oxford University Press, 1951, p. 407.
5 Moritz Schlick, *Problems of Ethics*, translated by David Rynin. New York: Dover Publications, 1962, p. 43. This short summary of Schlick's theory on free will is taken from pp. 143-58 of this work.
6 P. H. Nowell-Smith, *Ethics*. Baltimore: Penguin Books, 1954, esp. pp. 270-90.
7 C. S. Campbell, "Is Free Will a Pseudo-Problem?" *Mind*, LX (1951), esp. pp. 686-706.

CHAPTER II

1 J. P. Sartre, *L'Etre et le Néant*, quoted in G. Marcel, *The Philosophy of Existentialism*. New York: Citadel Press, 1961, p. 79.
2 Cf. Maurice Kahn Temerlin, "On Choice and Responsibility in a Humanistic Psychotherapy," *Journal of Humanistic Psychology*, Spring 1963, pp. 35-48.

3 Marc Oraison, *Vie Chrétienne et problèmes de la sexualité*. Paris: Lethiel-leux, 1952, pp. 98-197.

4 Immanuel Kant, *The Fundamental Principles of the Metaphysics of Ethics*, in J. A. Mann and G. F. Kreyche, editors, *Approaches to Morality*. New York: Harcourt, Brace and World, 1966, p. 195. This work is referred to in later chapters simply as *Approaches*.

5 Ibid., p. 199.

6 Georg W. Hegel, *The Spirit of Christianity*, in *Approaches*, p. 241.

7 St. Thomas Aquinas, *Summa Theologica*, I, q. 64, a. 2.

CHAPTER III

1 Cf. Schlick, *Problems of Ethics*, esp. pp. 79-99.

2 Cf. G. E. Moore, *Principia Ethica*. London: Cambridge University Press, 1959, esp. pp. 1-21.

3 Cf. A. J. Ayer, *Language, Truth and Logic*. New York: Dover Publications, 1936, esp. pp. 103-13.

4 W. Faulkner, Nobel Prize Address. Cf. Lawrance Thompson, *William Faulkner, An Introduction and Interpretation*. New York: Barnes and Noble, 1963, Appendix, p. 187.

5 Plato, *Timaeus*, 246 a 6 ff.

6 Aristotle, *Nichomachean Ethics*, 1106 636-1107 a.

7 Kant, *The Fundamental Principles of the Metaphysics of Ethics*, in *Approaches*, p. 195.

8 Johann G. Fichte, *The Vocation of Man*, edited by Roderick M. Chisholm. New York: Liberal Arts Press, 1956, esp. pp. 93-135.

CHAPTER IV

1 P. Romanell, *Toward a Critical Naturalism*. New York: The Macmillan Company, 1958; *Approaches*, p. 404. Cf. Chapter II, note 4.

2 Diog. Laert., *Lives of the Philosophers*, 10.

3 J. Bentham, *Introduction to the Principles of Morals and Legislation*, cc. 1-4.

4 A. Comte, *System of Positive Polity*, General Concl. to the Preliminary Discourse, I, pp. 329-30.

5 J. S. Mill, *Utilitarianism*, Ch. II.

6 W. T. Stace, *The Concept of Morals*. New York: The Macmillan Company, 1962, p. 163.

7 Plato, *Theaetetus*, #166.

8 T. Hobbes, *Leviathan*, cc. 1 and 2.

9 St. Thomas Aquinas, *Summa Contra Gentiles*, III, 117.

10 S. Kierkegaard, *The Sickness Unto Death*, translated by Walter Lowrie. New York: Doubleday and Company (Anchor Books), 1954, p. 165.

11 J. P. Sartre, *Le Sursis*, quoted in Marcel, *Philosophy of Existentialism*, p. 77.

12 Ibid., p. 87.

13 Ibid., esp. "Existence and Human Freedom," pp. 47-90.

14 F. Nietzsche, *Thus Spake Zarathustra*, Prologue, 4.

15 F. Nietzsche, *Beyond Good and Evil*, 259.

16 Cf. F. J. Thonnard, *A Short History of Philosophy*, translated by Edward A. Maziarz. New York: Desclée Company, 1955, p. 799.

17 Kratkii Filosoficheskii Slovar, "Morality," *Gozpolitizda*. Moscow: Gozpolitizda, 1942, p. 177.

18 William James, *The Will To Believe, and Other Essays in Popular Philosophy*. New York: Longmans and Company, 1897, esp. pp. 184-215.

19 John Dewey, *Reconstruction in Philosophy*. New York: Henry Holt and Company, 1920, esp. pp. 161-86.

20 Cf. Richard Hofstadter, *Social Darwinism in American Thought*. Boston: Beacon Press, 1955, p. 45.

21 H. Spencer, *Social Statics*. New York: D. Appleton and Company, 1864, p. 79.

22 I. Martkovich and Y. Pozanova, "New Law on Marriage and the Family," *Soviet Life*, Feb. 1969, No. 2 (149), pp. 6-8.

23 Alexander Sesonske, *Value and Obligation*. Fair Lawn, N. J.: Oxford University Press (Galaxy Books), 1964, p. 77.

CHAPTER V

1 Immanuel Kant, *Critique of Pure Reason*, 2nd ed., 4.

2 Immanuel Kant, *Groundwork of the Metaphysic of Morals*, in T. K. Abbott, *Kant's Theory of Ethics*, 6th ed. London: Longmans and Company, 1909, p. 18.

3 Ibid., p. 47.

4 Immanuel Kant, *Critique of Practical Reason*, in Abbott, *Kant's Theory of Ethics*, p. 218.

5 Ibid., p. 187.

6 Immanuel Kant, *Religion Within the Bounds of Reason Alone*, translated by T. M. Greene and H. H. Hudson. Glasgow: Open Court Publishing Company, 1934, p. 3.

7 Schlick, *Problems of Ethics*, pp. 100-19.

8 Kant, *Critique of Pure Reason*, 662.

9 Kant, *Critique of Practical Reason*, 233.

10 Immanuel Kant, *Opus Postumum*. Berlin Critical Edition, Vol. XXI, p. 12.

11 Ibid., p. 15.

12 Ibid., p. 104.

13 F. C. Copleston, *A History of Philosophy*. Garden City, N. Y.: Doubleday and Company (Image Books), 1960, Vol. 6, Pt. II, p. 133.

14 Cf. James Collins, editor, *Philosophical Readings in Cardinal Newman*. Chicago: Henry Regnery Company, 1961, Ch. XVIII.

15 Georg W. Hegel, *Philosophy of Right*, translated by T. M. Knox. Oxford: Clarendon Press, 1942, No. 135, pp. 89-90.

CHAPTER VI

1 S. Toulmin, *An Examination of the Place of Reason in Ethics*. London: Cambridge University Press, 1950, pp. 46-60.
2 Aristotle, *N. E.*, II, vi, 15.
3 St. Thomas, *S. T.*, I-II, q. 18, a. 5.
4 F. Suarez, *De bonit et Malit. hum. act.*, disp. 2, s. 2.

CHAPTER VII

1 H. Bergson, *The Two Sources of Morality and Religion*, translated by R. Ashley Audra and Cloudesley Brereton. New York: Henry Holt and Company, 1935, p. 75.
2 Ibid., pp. 19-22.
3 Ibid., pp. 26-28.
4 Ibid., p. 37.
5 Ibid., p. 90.
6 D. von Hildebrand, *Christian Ethics*. New York: David McKay Company, 1953, p. 90.
7 Ibid., p. 186.
8 Bergson, *Two Sources*, p. 78.

CHAPTER VIII

1 Ulpian, Tit. I, *De Jure et Justitia*, V.
2 Joseph Fletcher, *Situation Ethics: The New Morality*. Philadelphia: Westminster Press, 1966, p. 165.
3 Ibid., p. 37.
4 Ibid., p. 69.
5 Cicero, *De Republica*, III, xxii, 33.
6 The references to the teaching of St. Thomas on this subject are taken from *S. T.*, I-II, q. 94, arts. 1-5.
7 Genesis 22:2.
8 Exodus 12:35.
9 Osee 1:2.
10 Duns Scotus, *Commentaria Oxoniensia*, III, d. 37, nn. 5-8.
11 Cf. G. Biel, *Collectorium circa IV Sent.*, I, d. 17, q. 1, a. 3, con. 1, k.
12 H. Grotius, *De Jure Belli ac Pacis*, I, i, X.
13 S. Kierkegaard, *Fear and Trembling*, translated by Walter Lowrie. Princeton, N. J.: Princeton University Press, 1941, pp. 79-92.
14 St. Thomas, *S. T.*, I-II, q. 18, a. 9.
15 Cf. G. Morel, "Un athée absolu: Karl Marx," *Etudes*, fev. 1965, pp. 155-70.
16 Cf. Plato, *Laws*, 776 b5-c3.
17 Aristotle, *Politics*, 1255 a 1-3.
18 St. Thomas, *S. T.*, I-II, q. 94, a. 5, ad 3.

19 S. E. Stumpf, *Morality and the Law*. Nashville: Vanderbilt University Press, 1966, pp. 203-04.
20 Aristotle, *Rhetoric*, Bk. I, Ch. 13, 1373b 4.
21 Lon Fuller, *The Law in Quest of Itself*. Boston: Beacon Press, 1966, p. 114.
22 Hobbes, *Leviathan*, 1, 13.
23 J.-J. Rousseau, *Social Contract*, Bk. I, Ch. 1.
24 Cf. Isaiah Berlin, *Karl Marx: His Life and Environment* (Home University Library of Modern Knowledge). New York: Oxford University Press, 1948, p. 9.
25 G. Radbruch, *Rechtsphilosophie*, 4th ed. Stuttgaart: Koehler, 1950, pp. 352-55.
26 Immanuel Kant, *Metaphysic of Morals*, pt. I, *Metaphysical Elements of the Theory of Right*, introd. B.
27 Stumpf, *Morality and Law*, p. 189.
28 St. Thomas, *S. T.*, I-II, q. 91, a. 1.
29 Grotius, *De Jure Belli ac Pacis*, Prolegomena, #11.
30 R. von Jhering, *Der Zweck im Recht*, 1886, quoted in Brendan F. Brown, editor, *The Natural Law Reader* (Docket Series). New York: Oceana Publications, 1960, p. 87.

CHAPTER IX

1 David Hume, *A Treatise of Human Nature*. Garden City, N. Y.: Doubleday and Company (Dolphin Book), 1961, Bk. III, Pt. I, Sect. 1, p. 423.
2 Cf. H. A. Prichard, "Does Moral Philosophy Rest on a Mistake?" *Mind*, XXI (1912), pp. 487-99.
3 Cf. Philippa Foot, "Moral Arguments," *Mind*, LXVII (1958), pp. 502-13.
4 Cf. Schlick, *Problems of Ethics*, esp. pp. 79-99.
5 Toulmin, *Examination of the Place of Reason in Ethics*, esp. pp. 46-60.
6 Moore, *Principia Ethica*, Ch. 1.
7 St. Thomas, *S. T.*, I-II, q. 94, a. 4.
8 Ibid., a. 5.
9 E. Westermarck, *Origin and Development of the Moral Ideas*, 2nd ed. New York: The Macmillan Company, 1924, Vol. I, p. 396.
10 Ibid., p. 388.
11 Ibid., pp. 4-5.
12 1 Machabees 6:46.
13 St. Thomas, *S. T.*, II-II, q. 64, a. 7.

CHAPTER X

1 J.-J. Rousseau, *Emile*, IV, Everyman's Library, p. 52.
2 Aristotle, *Politics*, Bk. I, Ch. 2.
3 St. Augustine, *De Civitate Dei*, XV, 5.
4 St. Thomas, *S. T.*, II-II, q. 188, a. 8.

5 Ibid., I, q. 96, a. 4.

6 Hobbes, *Leviathan*, esp. cc. 12 and 17.

7 Rousseau, *Social Contract*, esp. Bk. I, Ch. 6.

8 Hegel, *Philosophy of Right*, esp. pp. 123-56.

9 Cf. Stumpf, *Morality and Law*, Ch. 2.

10 Ibid., pp. 156-66.

11 Fuller, *Law in Quest of Itself*, p. 136.

12 St. Thomas, *S. T.*, I-II, q. 95, a. 1.

13 Ibid., q. 90, a. 4, ad 4.

14 Ibid., q. 92, a. 1.

15 Ibid., q. 96, a. 4.

16 *Riggs v. Palmer*, Court of Appeals of New York, 115 N. Y. 506, 22 N. E. 188.

17 *United States v. Holmes*, U. S. Circuit Court, Eastern District of Pennsylvania, 1842, 1 Wall Jr. 1, Fed. Cas. 360, no. 15, 383.

18 B. N. Cardozo, *The Paradoxes of Legal Science*. New York: Columbia University Press, 1928, p. 46.

19 Cf. James, *Will To Believe*, esp. pp. 184-215. Cf. Chapter IV, note 18.

20 St. Thomas, *S. T.*, I-II, q. 96, a. 2.

21 Aristotle, *De Generatione Animalium*, Bk. II, Ch. 3, 736 a 24-737 a 17.

22 St. Thomas, *S. T.*, I, q. 118, a. 2, ad 2.

23 Cf. Denis Cavanagh, M.D., "Reforming the Abortion Laws," *America*, Apr. 18, 1970, pp. 406-11.

132

INDEX

CAMROSE LUTHERAN COLLEGE LIBRARY

BJ
1012
.M 317 / 21,068